Cheryl Reinhardt

Why Men Marry

Why Men Marry

Insights From Marrying Men

A.T. Langford

MasterMedia Limited
New York

Published 1995 by MasterMedia Limited

MASTERMEDIA and colophon are registered trademarks
of MasterMedia Limited.

Library of Congress Cataloging-in-Publication Data
Langford, A. T.
    Why men marry : insights from marrying men / A.T. Langford
        p.   cm.
    ISBN 1-57101-022-X (hardcover) : $18.95
    1. Marriage—United States. 2. Men—United States— Attitudes.
I. Title.
HQ734.L318   1995
306.81'0973—dc20   94–42508

Book design and electronic publishing by
Lynn & Turek Productions, New York

Manufactured in the United States of America

To

David Alexander Caruth

Contents

Acknowledgments

I would like to thank the following people for their assistance, enthusiasm, and steadfastness: Susan Stautberg and Diana Lynn of MasterMedia; Mary Holloway, Diana Jelinek, Rae Ann Hoffmann, Dagmar O'Connor, Nan Eliot, Bernard Burke, Mary Dustan Turner, Jane Erlich, Ed Lebar, Liz Ellerton, Charlotte Odgers Breese, Mark Sheldon, Diane Waller, Joan Lauback, Jason Runnels, Stephanie Faul, David McCabe, Jacqueline Quillen, Diana Foster, Peggy Wilkins, James Barron, Shelby Hall, Tara Joseph; and posthumously, Alice Everhart Langford and Winifred Ainslee.

And especially the men who graciously agreed
to be interviewed for this book.

—ATL

Introduction

As long as there are comedians there will be jokes about marriage, often based on outlandish stereotypes. Interest in the subject is never-ending. Who's married? Who's not? Who's engaged? We speculate about it at parties, during coffee breaks, and on talk shows. We marvel at seemingly mismatched couples: Why did she marry him? How did he get her? We follow wedding announcements in local newspapers—sections referred to as "girls sports" by one woman I know! Marriages of celebrities, royalty, and politicians have become an international pastime to be romanticized, glorified, trivialized by millions.

Many women would like to be part of these pictures but somehow aren't. I have divorced friends who haven't been married in years and single friends involved in countless relationships—none leading to a wedding ceremony. Their boyfriends are blamed for the demise of these couplings because they didn't pop the question so eagerly awaited. It has to be the man's fault. After all, don't men view marriage as a trap to be avoided at all costs? Aren't they're terrified by the very thought? Didn't the so-called battle of the sexes start with a woman's calculated desire to hook an eligible bachelor? That mind-set leads women to invest men with too much power and too much responsibility, thus making women needlessly more vulnerable and men less so.

I always rejected this gospel, convinced by my own experience that men are not much different than women when it comes to relationships: they want to marry and need love, companionship, and security as much as we do. Not that my point of view has been easy to convey, mind you, especially to a friend whose heart has just been stomped on by *that jerk*. But was he always? I remember when he wasn't. Wouldn't it be tempting to ring up the jerk and get his angle? Maybe he could provide enlightenment either about himself, her, or the dynamic between them. His account, if listened to, might prevent my pal from getting into the same pickle again and perhaps even set her on the path toward the resolution she seeks, I reasoned.

Yet seldom, if ever, are men queried about their real feelings about marriage, how they choose women, get involved in relationships, and decide to "take the plunge." Even the words used to describe men's "act of committing marriage" are pejorative. So I decided to take it on myself to ask them about "holy deadlock."

I compiled 27 questions *(see Appendix)* that formed the basis of my interviews. Some questions were my own, others were suggested by women equally as curious as I. Additional questions were contributed by marriage experts and one of the first men I interviewed. All told, I talked (for an average of three hours each) with sixty-three men between the ages of 24 and 68—single, married, divorced, widowed, cohabiting. I found them through friends, acquaintances, complete strangers; I talked to anyone who would talk to me and was pleasantly surprised by how quickly and willingly most men agreed to be interviewed. Speaking of strangers, I think that's one reason so many of my interview subjects shared their views so freely—that, and my assurances of anonymity (their real names, and sometimes their professions or where they live have been changed, without sacrificing any of the accuracy of what they said).

To ensure a realistic sampling, I searched for men who were distinctively different from each other. Yet, this is not a statistical survey nor is it a social scientific study; its anecdotal content is more like an amalgam of focus groups, because certain patterns became readily apparent and identifiable.

Those interviewed are short, tall, brunette, blond, going bald or getting gray and are of Hispanic, African, or European origin. Their religion, if they have any, runs the gamut— Jewish, Protestant, Catholic, Baptist, Buddhist. Likewise, income levels vary; some are unemployed or are students, others make a living as small-business owners, firefighters, senior executives, artists, sales reps, lawyers, musicians, food critics, athletes, police officers, journalists. They hail from regions far and wide—and include, for example, a gallery owner on Madison Avenue, a rancher in the Texas Panhandle, and a private investigator from San Francisco.

Their answers are thought-provoking and disarmingly candid. I found these men were surprisingly willing to expose idiosyncrasies and weaknesses with humor as well as irony. Granted, some were tense at the beginning of our conversation but slowly became more relaxed, revealing hidden emotions as they got into the questions and forgot about themselves; others told me they'd reexamined their thoughts in serious preparation for our interview.

Their intimate accounts show an evolving process that varies from man to man, but basically they make a conscious decision to marry (women don't trap them), they know the qualities desired in a partner, and they deliberately seek out the kind of woman they want to spend their lives with. They long for a love they can trust and for a commitment they can count on. When these elude them they're honest about why.

Independent research supports such disclosures. One study reports that 74 percent of single men in their 30s said they wanted to marry, compared to 64 percent of women. Seventy-one percent of men over 45 thought it was better to be married than to go through life single.[1] Men said they are tired of being alone and actively seek companionship. In fact, they're twice as likely as women to admit loneliness as a motivation for marriage.[2]

Men remarry more quickly after divorce. The median span between divorce and remarriage is 2.2 years for men and 2.5 years for women.[3] Men live twice as long when they're married.[4] They earn an average of 30.6 percent more than unmarried men[5] and are promoted more rapidly.[6]

Each man I interviewed also talks about the qualities he feels are important in a woman—and those that are not—and describes how he tests certain assumptions (does he really want "a girl just like the girl who married dear old Dad"?) and discards others until he designs a template of the woman he wants to be with and eventually marry. The woman he describes is *not* the model we see in television commercials or magazine ads: scintillating, sparkling, and chic. He wants a "real" woman, one who has the courage to be herself, who's intelligent, trustworthy, funny, and kind.

None of this happens in a vacuum. Men must contend with stereotypes, business, and family. Societal influences come into play and time pressures interfere. Yet each man balances outside persuasions with a strong personal conviction before he makes the decision to marry. Ultimately he's a consumer considering his options. He makes the choice best for him.

Why Men Marry is divided into thirteen chapters. The first eleven, based on the reasons most often cited for marrying, fea-

1. Battelle Human Affairs Research Institute, *Reuters,* September 5, 1990.
2. R.H. Bruskin and Associates, *UPI*, March 16, 1989.
3. *Adweek*, June 25, 1990, p.103.
4. Princeton University Study, *The New York Times,* May 15, 1990, Section C, p.6.
5. University of Michigan Survey, *The Associated Press,* November 14, 1990.
6. Federal Reserve Board Study, *Chicago Tribune*, September 28, 1989, Perspective Section, p.23.

ture the men's stories, delivered in their own words. I have chosen these particular accounts because they best represent and best articulate what other men have told me. It is important to note, however, that few men marry for one reason only; most are spurred by a combination of factors, but all marry for the reasons cited here.

The book's format changes in the final two chapters : Final Words and General Patterns. The former gives a more detailed breakdown of men's thoughts on women, sex, and money—and includes their carefully considered advice to women interested in matrimony. General Patterns takes a focus group approach by identifying assumptions that apply to a larger universe.

I encourage you to listen carefully as these men talk about marriage. Keep in mind they are not psychologists, great philosophers, or even famous—although some are well on their way. They are the kind of men we see every day; men who live down the street, men we get a glimpse of in a crowded train, men we sit next to in meetings. Men who have at last agreed to let us in on the one revelation only they can share: why men marry.

Why Men Marry

One

LOVE
"I didn't know she'd steal my heart."

"For love, of course" is the reason the majority of men cited for getting married. But it was a reason few found easy to discuss. They confidently confided about orgasms, childhood fears, long held fantasies. But love was difficult, a different kettle of fish altogether.

Some men squirmed in their chairs while others gazed into space, a faraway look in their eyes as if they were remembering a certain woman. They stammered, hemmed and hawed, or became philosophical. But eventually all came around in their own way, like the rowing coach who told me, "It was quite obvious that relationship was far and beyond anything I'd come across in a long time. One of those magical, falling in love kind of things. It just came very naturally. There so were so many good things about it. It was very intense, we were close very quickly. It worked. You meet someone and everything jibes. You don't want to be apart from her—she becomes a part of everything you do, all your thoughts. I knew at some point I was going to make a commitment."

At best love is hard to define. Until the 11th century it had no name, being first put into song and heart by troubadours traveling from castle to castle to entertain and linger with wives left home by husbands gone off to the Crusades. Ever since, poets have rhymed it, rappers have talked it, scientists have tried to measure it. While there is no precise explanation for love, descriptions abound. We all know what love is and recognize when it happens to us or to others. We can see it; we can certainly feel it; sometimes we can even taste it. One small-business owner describes love as "Bliss, the abyss…it's when two people really become so intimate, tumbling into a blissful abyss. That's the high. That's when you feel almost intoxicated…"

"But," he continued, "men aren't good about telling women they're in love. Men bore each other for hours sitting in bars blabbing about their girlfriend. They tell you they love this about her, that about her; words tumble out. Finally one guy will pipe up and say, 'Instead of telling me, why not tell her?' But you know we hate scrutiny, especially of our feelings and triply hate scrutiny by our beloved. A man in love wants to gush, but fears not being taken solely at gush value. His lover might take the opportunity to interrogate him. 'Well, you said you loved me more than any other woman, that those other women don't count. Well, *how many* other women were there?' That's tough on us. Few men have the confidence to navigate those rapids. They just freeze. I know I do."

A disc jockey said his definition of marriage is set to music in the song "When I Fall In Love." A painter suggested, "If you can swing a high level of romance out of it that's sustainable, go for it! Love in all its manifestations is one of the highest levels of experience offered to human beings. Marriage offers the opportunity to explore it."

Here's how men explain love's dynamics: "When people fall they have no direction. It's all internal. You can't control that. If you're in love with someone you're just in love. It's chemistry." Some classify it: "There are two types of love—mad passionate love and workful love. Mad passionate love is wonderful but often hides something fundamentally flawed. You're mad about someone and you both know something's wrong, but the romantic side is so strong you bury any problems. Workful love sounds like the most incredibly unromantic concept, but an element of mutuality develops after the flaws are exorcised out of the relationship."

No one interviewed was cynical about love, a little circumspect perhaps, but basically enthusiastic. Few had given up! Men reminisced about first loves but were content to leave the past alone. A man on his second marriage said, "The greatest love I ever had was in high school, a kind of puppy love job. I was the big jock; she was a cheerleader but I went off to college and she stayed. When we broke apart I was devastated. She's married now with kids. Some twenty years later I have deliberately kept my distance, staying away from reunions. Seeing her now would sour a wonderful memory."

But the present is full of promise once a lasting attachment is made: a freshly married 31-year-old remarked, "I found myself so in love. After awhile, there were just so many ways I could verbally or physically express it. I wanted her to know that it wasn't a temporal thing, that I felt seriously and wanted to continue forever. It was a natural culmination of all my feelings and I was surprised by how easily and quickly they came. It was so effortless; marriage didn't seem like an end, it seemed like a beginning."

For love, pure and simple, is why men place a gold band on her third finger, left hand. Three men now tell their stories: Justin O'Connor, 29, has been married for two years; Ken Cooper, 50, is engaged; and Alan Mosley, 39, is looking for the real thing.

JUSTIN O'CONNOR

Twenty-nine-year-old Justin is five feet seven inches tall, with sandy colored hair and green eyes. He grew up in the Bronx, got his bachelor of science degree at a local college, and now works for the New York City Department of Transportation as a grants administrator.

Justin was one of the least hesitant men I talked to. Enthusiastic and funny, he creates the impression that whatever he does, he does with humor, goodwill, and gusto. Justin wears wild shirts (mauve, blue, and pink striped over an X and O pattern, for example), loves board games, and prefers his rock 'n' roll loud.

His mother and father (both deceased) dated in Ireland but later moved to and married in New York. He is the youngest of their four children, three boys and a girl. Justin has a "honeymoon baby" who's 15 months old.

Justin's Surprise...

66 I thought Kathleen was a goody two shoes snob; she thought I was an alcoholic. We knew each other from work but hated each other pretty much on sight. When I left that job, moving to a building in a different part of town, so did Kathleen. We ended up on the same floor and since we didn't know anyone else, decided to do lunch. I thought Kathleen was good friends with someone I couldn't stand and didn't get why a woman like her could be friends with such a terrible person. During lunch I found out I was totally off base; she couldn't stand her either. WOW, wrong perception. That's how we started out, at this lunch—I didn't know she'd steal my heart.

I didn't think I was her type. I'd seen one of her big, husky, good-looking boyfriends and I was like, no way this is going to happen with me, this short little petite thing. But again, a misconception. After a few more lunches, I asked her to the San Gennero street fair, and on that warm June evening we clicked right then and there. I fell in love in three weeks.

So many friends were getting married around that time and, of course, were curious to find out if I ever thought about saying, 'I do.' I told them there wasn't anyone out there I could completely love. Then boom! Kathleen appeared. The whole thing just melted and jelled and I just knew. I'd *never* had this feeling before. About a month, later I flew to California for a family reunion and all I could think about was Kathleen. I kept telling anyone who would listen that I was going to marry her. I said, 'Trust me. You will be at my wedding, remember this.'

Kathleen is *the* woman for me. I'm not very good at explaining these things verbally, but in my other three serious relationships the thought of marriage never entered my head. There wasn't that click. I mean Kathleen and I knew the mutual support for each other was there. Nothing about her could hurt me, nothing would make me back out. Everything about her was...what I wanted.

She has brains, a sense of humor, and is a strong woman. Being blond and blue-eyed wasn't a requirement, although it's nice. My sister's a strong woman, so was my mother. I'm attracted to that kind of woman; I don't like whimpering take-care-of-me types. Seems Kathleen was always a go-getter: she started working in high school and after getting her present job, began law school. That was a few months after we started going out. She's the *perfect* woman. (I hope I'm not repeating myself too much.)

I knew she wouldn't live with me; she came from a proper Catholic family. You know, you live with your parents until you're married. Besides, she was only twenty minutes away by car. So we went away weekends to get the feel of what we were about. Three months later I said, 'Would you consider getting married while you're in law school?' And she answered, 'Yes.' So then I said, 'Hey, Kathleen, what if we got engaged, say, next summer?' She smiled and said, 'All right.'

In my heart *I knew* she would say yes. We got along so well and spent so much time with each other and with each other's families. We talked about everything under the sun and when we were apart, sent each other cards and little notes. My brothers said they could tell the first time I introduced her. Patrick said it was the look in my eyes. I didn't think I was acting any different; I was just happy to be with her. If you don't love somebody, there is no reason to get married. We married a year later, had our wonderful daughter, and Kathleen graduates from law school soon. Can you believe all this in two years!**"**

KEN COOPER

Fifty-year-old Ken wears glasses and his mustache is turning gray, although his hair remains dark brown. An art dealer, he grew up in the Midwest. After graduating from Ohio State with a bachelor's degree in fine art, he set up a gallery in Indianapolis, but returned to his hometown of Cleveland where he has remained for the last twenty-five years.

The first thing I noticed about Ken was that he was dressed in dark colors and was very intense. He's fastidious and precise and doesn't waste a movement, or a word—everything is planned. He told me he eats eight strawberries, not five or nine, every morning for breakfast with his muesli and yogurt; and I'm not exactly surprised.

Ken's parents are dead; he's the oldest of three children and has two younger sisters. He is engaged.

Ken's Recovery...

❝ The questions for me were: a) Do you love this woman? b) Do you want to be with her? Part of me thinks of love as sparks flying. Seeing fireworks when she enters a room. What's love? I can tell you—Liz is the *only* person I can imagine spending the rest of my life with.

A month ago the thought of getting married meant panic, this week it means endless possibilities because we've grown together so much as a couple. I was frightened of getting married. Now it's not as important to be absolute about it. I focus on Liz, on my feelings about her, and the time we spend together. How *good* it is. It's a leap of faith.

Especially if I think about my experience with marriage. I was married for ten years and after that was quite reluctant to make another commitment. In the space of eleven months, my dog died, my dad died, my wife and I separated and went into marriage counseling. Then my mother died and we divorced. It was horrendous.

During marriage counseling I was absolutely convinced we'd get back together. I fell in love all over again, which made it even more difficult when it didn't work out. After the divorce I had this sense of, why put yourself through this shit? I felt sorry for myself. It took probably six months before I stopped believing I was never going to get into a long commitment again. Strangely I didn't have any desire to go out and be wild and crazy and play the field. I guess there was a certain sense of being vulnerable and feeling so hurt that I was conscious of not wanting to use somebody. I was feeling used myself and didn't want to do something for momentary release.

During that first year, a lot of my real values surfaced. I spent as much time with close friends as I did dating. In the divorce I lost a really wonderful place, so I put most of my energy into creating a new space in which to live and work. Those mornings I didn't have to leave for the airport, I headed out to the park, running and sweating, just to get my head straight, to get back into the world.

I decided after being with my ex-wife, who was quite passive and submissive, I wanted someone quite the opposite—a woman with a real sense of herself who had some depth, some soul, and wasn't shallow. I didn't want to be tempted into another relationship I could dominate. I wanted a woman who not only knew what she wanted, but would tell me. Nobody can read anybody else's mind, so why play guessing games? You'd be surprised how few people can tell you what they really want. Clearly I wanted someone who understood independence, who had friends of her own, and wasn't threatened when I needed quiet time. As much as I value being in a relationship, I don't think one person can be everything for the other.

I started out with Liz slowly. We were friends months before our first date. There was this flash, a real excitement at seeing her, being with her. About a year ago I asked her to marry me. We were having some problems, most of which centered on her anxiety over my lack of commitment. Liz wanted me to make up my mind so she could relax and worry about everything else! She's never been married.

Now we have to figure out how to live in the same city— we've been having a long distance relationship since Liz left Cleveland four years ago. After her job was cut back, she was hired by a multinational with offices all over the East Coast. I have been up and down searching for an appropriate place to settle. New York is too expensive, Washington's not bad. We thought about Boston but it's not a town for selling my kind of art. I looked through my files and found the name of another dealer, called him up and questioned him about the market. He spends 98 percent of his time out of Boston and has a failed marriage to prove it. That's not going to be me. I haven't given up trying to relocate; I've met a few potential clients but haven't sold a thing.

I'm trying my best to persuade Liz to return to the Midwest. There's plenty to do in this town, we could buy a huge Victorian house for the price of a two bedroom apartment in the East. She could have a garden, a dog, a more relaxed lifestyle. I'll make up the salary differential by working harder. Liz is extremely special to me, I trust her implicitly, and have enormous respect for her. Is that love? Sounds pretty good to me."

ALAN MOSLEY

Thirty-eight-year-old Alan has deep blue eyes and blondish hair that's gradually disappearing from the top of his head. After getting a B.A. in economics, Alan spent ten years in the film business before becoming a mortgage broker on Wall Street. However, he's about fed up with the long hours and the crowded office, where the person nearest him is only inches away.

Alan doesn't even fit the image of a hardened trader. He's sensitive, easygoing, thoughtful. He laughs a lot and likes to cook. He and his roommate share a loft with a large, open kitchen stocked with gadgets you see in gourmet stores. While we were talking he made taramasalata, the Greek appetizer.

His parents have been married for more than forty years and have two sons and a daughter. Alan is the middle child and single.

Alan's Dilemma...

" I'm 38 and still single. People ask me, 'Why aren't you married?' I'm not sure of the true reason anymore. There are so many different factors, so many things I've convinced myself of and even made up, that I can give you any number of pat answers.

I guess I always thought I'd get married and still do. When I was in high school, I was dating a girl whose parents were happily married and still in love with each other after having five children. The way they dealt with each other and talked, I could sense how enamored they were. Of course, they forgot about the kids sometimes so I guess you need a balance, but that's the way I'd like marriage to be for me.

People get married for the wrong reasons: to get out of the house, for money, for security. Guys marry right out of college, especially the sports guys I played ball with. My theory is that they were so accustomed to having a group around, they married not to be alone. I know one guy who married because he got a job as an insurance agent and needed a wife to help him entertain; another married because he wanted a mother for his kids.

I'd marry for love. I'd be so in love, I'd want that person to share all her love with me. If you've ever been in love, you know what it's about and how it feels. I hope I never *settle* for anything less. And I don't think that's any bullshit excuse. In the last few years I've learned the difference between falling in love and falling in infatuation. I have seen enough people calling infatuation 'love.' They meet and marry in a matter of weeks. Nothing can prevent them! Six months, maybe a year later, it wears off—they separate or divorce. It takes time to discover if it's *really* love.

I don't think my parents should have married each other. When Mother first came over from Denmark, she didn't speak English. She almost became hysterical when my father popped the question. She ran to my aunt sobbing about some woman named Mary. My aunt quietly commented, 'Are you sure he didn't say marry?' Great story, huh? They had a strong attraction but didn't know each other very well. I think she wanted to stay in the U.S.; he was taken with her beauty. They didn't have much in common then and don't to this day. For instance, my mother is outgoing and social; my father's idea of entertainment is weeding the garden. They stuck it out because of us kids.

If you really love somebody that feeling doesn't disappear. I know it must, but I guess I'm somewhat of a romantic, thinking love will last. I mean, I could easily become infatuated but I know myself well enough that...no, I wouldn't rush out and get married.

There were two women in my life I would have wedded had things broken my way. The first woman I loved needed to finish college; I was out and ready, but her parents were against it. They came from a pretty substantial background and since I wasn't a member of the right country club, sent her to Bermuda for the summer to stay with their social friends. She took the bait; when she returned, things weren't the same. The second woman I was in love with wasn't in love with me.

On the other hand, I've disentangled myself from a couple of long relationships because I didn't see any future. I went out with one woman steadily for almost two years, but didn't pursue marriage because I just didn't love her *enough*. Plus she wanted to be with me every night and every weekend, and that kept me from doing anything on my own.

I know what love is, that closeness and connection; if I never had it again, that would be awful. So I keep going. I meet women mostly through friends or chance circumstances. I've had so many blind dates I feel like Ray Charles! I met a woman on an Outward Bound trip who introduced me to a friend of hers in New Orleans. I like to get to know somebody on the telephone first—there's none of that prejudice about how we look. Most times I'll say, 'Let's meet.' Then excitement starts; you find out whether you're right for each other.

Like with the woman from New Orleans. We yammered on the phone for two weeks and the next thing I knew I'm flying there for a date. It was so intriguing, so much fun that I got into this fantasy, caught up in the thrill of romance. But I *knew* it was infatuation.

I wasn't what she expected. Clarice was looking for someone very smart like a doctor. On the phone I come across smart but I'm also playful; I don't want to be serious or aggressive all the time. Lately I've been trying to kick back a little bit, so I said, 'You take over. It's your town, I don't need to be in control here.' She wanted me to take charge of everything—where to eat, where to go, what to see. And I didn't want to, so we didn't exactly hit it off. I saw her a second time when I returned to visit my Outward Bound friend. I called, just for the hell of it, to say I was going to be in town and she started out with, 'Maybe we can get together for part of Saturday.' Then it was drinks Friday night and more of Saturday, then stay at my place for the whole weekend.

I slept with her and I'm not sure what the matter was, but at 28, Clarice wasn't very experienced. She said she'd never had a serious relationship. I tried to make her feel as comfortable as I could—she was more than just a fling. The whole thing was an experience, an intrigue, and certainly not boring.

Do I regret it? Not at all. I just opened my American Express bill and thought, 'My God! Hundreds of dollars in phone calls and flights.' It was great. We had fun but we never really connected. Clarice had different goals and was looking for somebody or something. But ah, the idea of romance got to me…I think or hope she liked me as a person. I spoke to her the other day and she told me about some doctor.

As I get older, I know what I *don't* want—I'm getting picky, picky, picky. I've been in situations where there's no obvious reason why a relationship couldn't work but I pushed the woman away. I'm intuitive enough to know when it's real, when it's right and when it's time. I allow myself to get close, but not too close. Because I have a little of my father in me, I don't want to marry for infatuation. We're all such creatures of habit. I'm careful, but when I fall so quickly sometimes I'm trying to convince myself 'Well, this time infatuation will turn into something more meaningful.' But I don't convince myself much, that's why I'm not married. In the long run, I'm too pragmatic about love.**"**

Two

EQUAL PARTNERSHIP
"It's gotta be 50:50 or nothing."

"It's a partnership. You decide you've been out in the world long enough, sampled all the wines and picked the vintage you think is okay. It's time to build assets..." concluded one financial advisor.

Straight and to the point, partnership is the second reason men cited for marrying. "It's like a game of catch," a man twice married said. "In its most idyllic form, marriage is a partnership, a close union in which your first passionate interest is each other. I admire people who are good at it."

A sculptor pointed out, "Marriage is a lifelong partnership basically. You're with someone to enjoy the good times and help in the bad times. But I'm not sure that women look at marriage as an equal partnership, which is where security and money become important."

Men want to share their lives and want a woman they can rely on, to take some of the emotional and financial load off, to divide up household duties, to contribute to their personal growth, to have fun with.

A few men gave me ratios—50:50 or 45:55—depending on the abilities of each. A bachelor explained, "We make up a list of things to get done, figure out who can do what better, what neither of us can do and, if we have the money, what we can pay someone else to do. Like hanging wallpaper: I'm not good at it—if my partner is, then she does it."

Men in the arts or freelancers working at home are more flexible when it comes to sharing in traditional "woman's work"—cleaning, doing the laundry, picking up the kids from school, like Mr. Mom. Men are inching toward the kitchen. Dad's Saturday pancake breakfast is ready for prime time, with a "we all gotta eat, don't we?" attitude.

One newly married man, told by his wife that her job was quickly becoming obsolete, gave her confidential information she wouldn't ordinarily have access to, thereby enabling her to move on. He said he just wanted her to be happy and couldn't stand seeing her bored and frustrated. Marriage as partnership is its own ecosystem.

As one entrepreneur told me, "Marriage has to be one of the toughest things you do in your life, and the *only* way to make it work is to look at it as a joint venture. You support each other based on mutual respect. If I come home one day and casually mention to my wife, 'I'd like to dress up in women's clothing,' the answer I would hope to get is, 'Well, that's wonderful, dear, let's go shopping.' In other words, you just want to be supported. Each has to be willing to support the partnership by balancing out each other's strengths and weaknesses." Marriage as a partnership means traveling through life with an ally.

A management trainee defined marriage as "a team effort. You both work toward goals, whether it's raising a family, being active in your community, or having a happy, productive career. But at the same time, you enjoy life and grow old together." Continuing the sports metaphor, a Texan explained, "Marriage is a basketball game. It's helping each other out when your back is against the wall. If one guy is a little tired and you need the extra point, you both develop a play for him. He stays away from the rim because he may not have enough energy to make the shot. When you're a team, you have to adjust when there's a problem—but I think couples forget that."

When asked what they would give up by *not* being married, almost all the men interviewed said having the opportunity for "the good things, like companionship." Men like the idea of having an equal around, someone capable and willing to share joint responsibilities.

A divorced small-business owner says, "To me, marriage is a business proposition between two people. It's a legally binding union. You have to share everything and if you have a couple of kids, it becomes a family business. It is also a place where you agree to work out your differences and prepare to grow with each other. Both get something out of it. Why else are you getting together? You help her; she helps you. You make decisions together."

A television actor has a more romantic concept of partnership: "Marriage is two people conspiring to make each other's lives better, to bring out the best in each other, to support each other and just take care of each other through the good and the bad."

In the following few pages Andrew Montgomery, dating at 29, and Zack Tillani, married for twelve years at 37, and Emmett Sherman, remarried at 42, discuss "taking a *partner* from this day forward."

ANDREW MONTGOMERY

Twenty-nine-year-old brown-haired, brown-eyed Andrew graduated from an Ivy League college, became an investment banker and was transferred to London, where he finished his MBA at the London School of Economics. In 1992 he left the world of finance, took time to recover, recharge, and "contemplate his navel" before starting a second career in an international entertainment company.

Andrew delivers his lines with an almost poker-faced seriousness. I can visualize him on the stage, dressed in a dinner jacket, hand in his pocket—very Noel Cowardish. He even looks and acts a bit like him—clever, funny with a pinch of brittleness. When not making the world safe for American films and television, he skis, plays tennis, and rides.

His parents have been married for thirty-seven years. Both run their own businesses. Andrew, the younger of their two sons, is single.

Andrew's Test...

❝ It sounds rather odd, but at one point in my life I was told to quit my job and get a girlfriend. I was so stressed out. My doctor surmised I hated my job and was lonely. He was half right. Literally about two weeks later, I was at a dinner party and met a woman. That's when I said, 'She'll do...next?' I woke up a few months later thinking, 'What have I done?' At least I didn't marry her. She was the first 'bus' that came along and I jumped on. For God's sake, it was going to hell but I forgot to read the sign in front.

I was in finance for a half dozen years, impersonating an investment banker. They kept paying me more and more money. It was ridiculous. I was 27, being paid six figures to tell people twice my age how to run their companies. It was just a load of crap and I couldn't take it any longer. I worked twenty hour days, slept, went to the gym, and gave up my social life. I was on call twenty-four hours, like a doctor. In the midst of all this I had the great revelation, so I sold the house, sold the car, sold the horse, and a few things in between, and moved in with divorced friends.

They kidded me all the time about having the obligatory first marriage, so I could join their 'club.' Their divorces seemed to fall into three categories: they married quickly; married too young—before they were fully formed—or they got engaged and were too weak to back out.

The ones who married too quickly were the most common. They married before the initial euphoria had worn off and were sorely disappointed when it did. They hadn't taken what I call 'the breakfast table test.' You have to imagine sitting across from the woman you're seeing *every morning for the next fifty years*. Pass that test and you've got a chance.

The ones who married young are a different story. People change at different rates and it's great if you change when your partner does, but the odds are against it if you're young. You change a lot; that's where the trouble starts. Say you suddenly decide that you want to run off to Paris, live in a garret, and paint bad murals. It's rather difficult to do that the weekend after you get married, especially if your spouse is all set to start her job at the law firm.

I can't imagine being married young, knowing what I know now. Men change between 25 and 30. I'm still not settled enough about my life or my ambitions and I'll be 30 soon. You have to get certain things out of your system first, unless you find the kind of partner who'll be happy living in that garret.

I have friends who divorced after six months of marriage. They knew there were fundamental problems and differences between them, but stuck their heads in the sand. After all, they'd been engaged for over a year and a wedding was *expected*. Neither had the courage to call the whole thing off.

When I think of marriage, a team thing, a partnership, a mutual support system comes to mind. I want someone who can hold her own; independent and strong-minded. I can't imagine being married to a woman with whom I share all the same friends, all the same interests, welded at the hip, forever being invited everywhere as a couple. I look at it as two people living very tight, parallel lives, sort of nudging into each other but not crossing or twined around each other. It's not that I don't enjoy spending time with my partner, but I think to keep things permanently fresh you must have different interests. The most successful marriages I've seen are the ones where the husband and wife do their *own* thing.

Consequently, I have never understood the rather futile custom of women taking their husband's name, that whole identity thing. I would not want to impose my identity on someone else. That ritual of becoming Mrs. Andrew Montgomery. What about the woman underneath? She doesn't even have her Christian name banging about. It doesn't appeal to me.

I was in one situation where the woman I was with just wanted to exist for me—and that was it. Everywhere I turned, she was either picking up after me or folding my clothes or pouring me a cup of coffee. You know everyone jokes about becoming the perennial bachelor, set in your ways? Well, I knew I'd had it when she rearranged my spice cupboard. I like to cook. There's a lot of love and art and math and science in it. I free myself when I cook. So when she took it upon herself to *un*alphabetize my fifty spices, I found it damned unattractive.

I would rather not be in a relationship than be in a bad relationship, which took me a long time to figure out. Finally I was able to *not* be in a relationship for over a year. I saw all sorts of nice women but never took anything further than a few nights out. I broke my habit of going out with what I call 'wounded women,' people who have just broken out of relationships and who I occasionally caught on the rebound. They were fairly safe and I was quite happy to give, of course, but then I had to be careful about being used. Now I look for reciprocity when it's my turn; the other party must hold up her side. Going back to the cooking analogy, if I cook, she washes up. But if she wanted to cook, I'd be happy to wash up.

Male and female roles have changed in the last twenty years. The man can't say he'll provide for the family of 2.3 children. Thinking like that doesn't exist anymore. I would marry someone who I thought could do as well as I can. I want to walk into a relationship on an equal footing. We might not be rich at the beginning but at least we could try to make it together—more fun than marrying someone with goblets of money.

Although men say they want to marry rich women, I know very few who can survive being kept by a 'trust fund baby' (a woman who has family money). Men are much more defined by their jobs. When it comes down to it, I'd rather be with someone who made it on her own and who has control of her finances, of her life.

I wish more marriages were partnerships but in most I've observed, one party tends to dominate, like 70:30. I think the most interesting ones sit around 50:50, but shift back and forth depending on what's going on.

I'm in one like that now with Karen. It's not easy at times. Neither one of us is willing to subsume our personality, our own particular goals, or our ambitions. Nor do we want to be apart; so we work it out. It takes coordination because she keeps different hours than I do, sometimes working weekends. But at least we're in related fields so I understand. Neither one of us is looking at this relationship as a six-month project. There's a fixed point out there with more than fifty years written on it. Clearly Karen passed the breakfast table test! Now we're organizing for the short term. The next step is cohabitation.**"**

ZACK TILLANI

Thirty-seven-year-old Zack is slim, has a small face with sharp features, and dark hair and eyes. He was born in south Boston, went to MIT on a scholarship, and graduated from Harvard Business School. He lives and works in southern California where he publishes and buys small magazines for a large conglomerate.

Downtime doesn't exist for Zack. When not at his office, he's bench pressing at the gym—five days a week—and on weekends, he's racing his twelve-speed bike around the countryside or gardening. He's directed, planned, and determined. Zack affects being laid back, but I could have sworn I heard his fingers drumming on the table.

Zack's parents are married; he's their only child.

Zack's Graduation...

❝ I've been married for twelve years today. It's hard to believe Lorna and I have been married *that* long, the time has gone by so fast, but I guess everyone says that.

We were in some of the same classes at business school and dated on a steady basis, but I could foresee that coming to a halt with graduation approaching. We were both frantically interviewing for jobs; however, not in the same geographical areas. We made a deal: if I could make more of a commitment, she would agree to interview in cities I was considering. So I did and you know, as much as I liked my independence, making a relatively small compromise to be with Lorna wasn't so mind-boggling.

I always wanted to be in a dual-career marriage; I don't find dependence attractive. I wanted somebody who was happy on her own terms. Lorna had enough independence and self-determination to have her own life; besides, she's good-looking, intelligent, and loves me. I found that quite startling. I guess I'm like Groucho Marx: I wouldn't want any woman who'd want me, possibly because I'm not the easiest person to get along with—difficult, selfish, exacting.

I married for love and companionship, but believe me, economics and lifestyle were carefully considered. I was looking for a career-oriented woman. At least I was in the right place—at *B* School—to begin my search, if that's what you'd call it. I started dating in junior high, so I knew the qualities I wanted. Next I narrowed down the field, then found what was available versus my 'perfect' image. I had eventually planned to settle down, to build a life and grow together with this anonymous woman. I expected to be married at some point in time, a tradition I got from my Roman Catholic parents. Although not desirable, I considered the possibility that I wouldn't marry;

that I might not find anyone capable of living up to my expectations or anyone who could tolerate me. Then I met Lorna.

In retrospect, I'm not sure I ever asked Lorna officially. I couldn't get the words out; I never said, 'Will you marry me?' I bought the ring, gave it to her, and said, 'I thought you might like this.' After I gave her the ring, we set a date. Actually, I guess the whole thing was, well, strange. I called her father to ask him for the name of his jeweler and a little later, Lorna's mother called, hinting around, 'Is there something I should know?' Needless to say, my wife was surprised—I hadn't mentioned anything yet!

You know, I thought marriage would be constraining, full of tradeoffs, but being married to Lorna all these years has really enhanced my life. Sure, there were times when we wanted to put an end to it—most couples have moments like those—but our problems were never *that* serious. After twelve years we're still together; Lorna is a marketing whiz, we have a small daughter, and my career is going well. Marrying a woman who is my equal, a true partner, was key for me.**"**

EMMETT SHERMAN

Forty-two-year-old Emmett looks like Jerry Seinfeld except he's bigger and barrel-chested. He grew up in Michigan, has two degrees (a bachelor of arts and a master of social work), and has been on the sales force of a number of organizations in and around Minneapolis–St. Paul. When we spoke, he was talking to headhunters and has since found another job.

Emmett is no doubt talented at sales because he's convincing, friendly, and solid. I got the feeling he'd know the most minute detail about whatever product or service for which he's responsible. He's also good at making things work—stubborn pieces of wood turn into shelves, machines hum, even his beloved basketballs find their way into the basket under his guidance.

His parents have been married "for ages" and have three children, Emmett and two daughters. Emmett remarried two years ago.

Emmett's Definition...

❝ My expectation of marriage is absolute; I need a clear partnership. I don't want the full burden of income, the full burden of the household chores, the full burden of creating the fun. I don't want to be the one responsible for keeping the lines of communication open, solving problems, initiating sex. It has to be a joint effort.

Maybe I got this idea growing up. Both my mother and father worked. My father was not a great businessman and believe me, I see a similar arrogance. But I'm getting ahead of myself.

Let me tell you about the difference between my first and second marriages. This first so-called 'partnership' was a burden because Becky wanted me to take care of her. That included doing almost everything; earning most of the income, doing the cooking and laundry, even typing and handing out fliers for her first exercise business. I went so far as to put those damn leaflets under car windshields! I thought I was being supportive until I took a good look at what was happening.

Becky had a pretty good life—she flew back home to see her parents at least four times a year, did some work there, took a month off in the summer. She was a dancer, so professionally she had the flexibility (no pun intended). I didn't. I had to hold down a job to keep it all going. Becky spent money but didn't bring much in. That had a devastating effect on what I had originally perceived as a partnership. I backed off. I started doing less and less, which led to increased fighting over what *I* wasn't doing.

We had bitter arguments over what a 'partnership' meant. Then the affection and love went. So she sought affection elsewhere. I am not even sure she got what she wanted. You know, she drove off with the other guy in a car my family lent me.

My father offered it to me when he could no longer drive. She asked for it and got it in the divorce settlement.

I remarried in 1990, six years after the divorce. I fulfilled my dream by finding my current relationship—a real partnership. It's very different from my first marriage. I have a partner who is hard-driving and quite successful. Diane is an absolutely fabulous cook and has an excellent vision of space. She worked with the architect in designing our bedroom, the kitchen, and bathrooms. And not to put too fine a point on it, she's also a very good lover and thinks sex is real important. She insists on it.

It took me six years to find her. I dated anybody. I asked all sorts of women out to see if anyone would want to be with me. I had to reestablish my own sense of being, my manhood. It was a rebuilding process. I wasn't hunting for a spouse.

I found myself physically attracted to women with great legs and asses. Big breasted women or blondes weren't for me. As for character, I wanted someone who was stable, solid, had a sense of fairness, and was self-sufficient. I figured all this out the way successful business men and women will tell you how they got to the top—because they failed plenty of times. You learn from your mistakes if you pay attention.

I was involved with another woman before I met Diane. It was pretty intense; we talked about marriage, but I felt she wasn't good partner material. Too much 'princess' behavior. I had this gut feeling that down the line she'd give up her job. It wasn't a good time for me in my career: I didn't feel capable of supplying all the money. You know I always go back to that picture of women I grew up with. My sisters have always been working partners, so was my mother. I didn't want a wife staying at home, taking care of the kids, moaning, 'That's *all* I can do.'

Even though I was seeing this other woman, I kept on looking around. I wasn't myopic. That's how I met Diane. We lived on the same block and I picked her up. Our volleyball team needed another player so I asked her if she would play with us.

I had watched her for about a month and was just waiting for an opportunity to say more than 'Hello. My name is…'

I gotta tell you, I have a great partner. Of course there were some ups and downs the four years before we married. We lived together for a year. I tested her. We had fights, I'd stomp away then come crawling back. We'd both cry on the street and ask each other, 'Do you love me? Do you care about me?' I wasn't testing her for marriage; I was testing for love, for trust, for nurturing.

Diane stuck by me although she saw me in a very bad light because of my jobs. Financially and career-wise I was not together at all, struggling. You have no idea how difficult it was. But she stuck by me. I didn't think she'd make a good partner, I knew she would—our experiences together proved that. We've been married for two years now and I couldn't be happier.**"**

Three

FAMILY
"Who says we don't have biological clocks?"

Much has been made of women's biological clocks: how women become frantic to find a father for their unborn child; how time starts to run out once we hit our late 30s; how a certain broodiness begins to set in. Tick, tick, tick. Like the crocodile who swallowed the timepiece in Peter Pan, the fear follows us around. Ah, but men too have time frames that are biological in a sense. Men reach a phase in life when they're pressured to produce a little Wendy or John and give up playing Peter Pan.

A newly married man told me, "I'm beginning to feel I'm behind a lot of my peers, now that most of my close friends are married and working on their second or third child. I wish the timetable were not so competitive. There's enough of that in the office."

Thus, the third reason men marry: to have a family. I found it absolutely amazing that many men mentioned children positively. I had expected to hear the usual rug-rat, cookie-crumbler, curtain-climber diatribe; I kept waiting for complaints about the expense or the inconvenience of having kids, but I didn't hear much of it.

A recent father did caution, "Children are the most dangerous thing to any partnership. They are time consuming, cumbersome, and take away all the attention. They change the whole dynamic of your relationship. So anyone who wants children should first have a viable marriage because having children is a risk."

A bachelor said if his girlfriend met him at the door with, "Hello, darling, I'm pregnant," he'd stand by her decision, and if that was to have the baby, marriage would fit into the equation. "I'm *not* a great believer in single-parent families," he said. "I don't think society knows what to do. It's hard enough for two people to raise one child. It isn't a bad reason to get married. If it happens and the whole thing looks fairly sensible—well, I mean, there are certainly worse reasons. I think it is very brave when people who know they shouldn't get married go ahead—so the baby will have two parents."

A briefly married 40-year-old cited children as his *only* reason to remarry. "I would have the expectation of being a good husband and father. A good one, not a mediocre one. Of course, I'd have to take better care of myself and pay more attention to my business so I could make enough money."

And a 32-year-old sales rep said, "I think the whole point of marriage is to have children. You create a family unit. Of course I do have the fantasy of the perfect children, the private school, the nanny, but even if I did have a child with some sort of birth defect, I am sure I could cope with that too."

A 54-year-old reflected on the reason he married his ex-wife. "All of my married friends had children. I was visiting one with a new baby. The kid was taking a nap in his bed and I tentatively put my arm around him. He smelled so good, like baby powder with a sort of innocence, this blond, blue-eyed angel. I decided right then and there I wanted one of my own. I had this strong paternal instinct, which maybe a lot of men don't have."

Women with children, especially young children, were viewed favorably. One man in his 40s told me he had a fantasy about marrying a woman with a small child; another talked about spending the summer with a girlfriend who had a small baby and realizing how grounded he felt, for the first time in years. Someone else's children exert a strong influence. One man confided, "I'm with Anita because of her family. My parents are dead and I'm an only child. I looked at her and at her children as the family I don't have. Believe me, that whole setup had a pretty strong pull."

Even a bachelor about town was won over by his lover's offspring. "I didn't know much about children. But there is much to know. I remember the evening I started to climb out of my ignorance. The children were little, two and five years old. They had come over for dinner with their mother. All of a sudden it was like ear plugs were removed. I could understand what they were saying. I told my shrink what happened. He said it was because I wasn't defending myself against them."

Men who are interested in starting a family naturally look for women who fit their criteria. A 38-year-old confided about dating a woman he knew wasn't right for him: "Oh my God, she couldn't be the mother of my children. She'd forget them; she'd go to the grocery store and leave them at the checkout counter!" Another said loving children is like loving pets, that women who complain about a few dog hairs on his sofa turn him off.

Men are excited by the prospect of having a child. Different pictures snap to mind: the father-to-be pacing outside the hospital waiting room, cigars crowding his pocket; a husband dressing in operating room greens and calmly uttering reassurances to his wife, in between taking breaths with her. Then dad with the video camera...

A 32-year-old marveled, "Having a child is a thrill. It concentrates my mind. It blows me away. Any day now, me with a baby! You know I looked at my parents, particularly last weekend when three of us kids came back with spouses, and I saw how happy we made them. That's what it's all about—family.

Others not yet married plan how it will be. I will be different from my father who thought all he had to do was put cash on the kitchen table and everything would be fine. I'll be more interactive in the family process, take the kids to school, fix their lunch, coach the soccer team. I see men I work with who have successful careers and good families. Maybe men have finally found out we can do both."

We'll hear next from three men who say family is their reason for tying the knot. Meet Jay Dunbar, single, Cody Smith, just married, and Jackson Leslie, married for nine years with a two-year-old daughter.

JAY DUNBAR

Thirty-eight-year-old Jay is blond. His watery blue eyes are almost lashless and his crisply trimmed mustache and beard are straw-colored—even the lens in his horn-rimmed glasses have a beige tint. He attended private boarding schools, and after graduating from college, became a professional violinist before obtaining a masters in international economics.

Jay makes his living as a business writer, reporting on subjects as varied as the heroin trade in the Golden Triangle or the sale of human body parts in Pakistan. He now lives in the nation's capital, and I got the impression he's really into being part of the media scene.

His parents have been married forty years. Jay is the oldest of their three children and single.

Jay's Plans...

" Actually, I'm almost *eager* to get married. To love someone, to have her love me, and then to have children is one of the deepest experiences life has to offer. I know about kids—my ex-fiancée has two small sons. Believe me, those little boys were quite a handful. I'm fairly confident I understand how to raise children now.

My relationship with Charlotte opened me up to the idea of getting married. I was *really* happy when we first got engaged; in retrospect, it happened too soon. We had known each other for a couple of years and after her marriage broke up, we had a brief affair that didn't amount to much. Afterward we sort of drifted around each other. One day I woke up and realized I didn't like the idea of her going out with anybody else. Six months later we were engaged. We were still in 'the romantic part' and hadn't really begun to negotiate our way through key issues like Charlotte's having more children or separate bank accounts.

I thought we could work all this out over the course of our engagement but we couldn't even settle on where we would live. I wanted to buy a larger apartment in town; she wanted a house in the suburbs. I think she wanted to get engaged partly to be married again and partly to resolve her kids' problems. One was very troubled at seeing his mother with me or any man. I mean, his father had left. Right? I was aware of what I was getting into, I knew the divorce rate for second marriages is 60 percent, often because of stepchildren. I said, 'Yes, let's build a life together. I'll help you with your sons and you can help me with whatever it is I need.'

We were caught in this passionate, unhappy dance. Charlotte would take the ring off her finger, march out of my apartment in a huff, then come back and put the ring on. After a few performances like that, I put the ring back in the box and shut it away in a drawer, where it is today.

We decided to take a six-month break. Of course, we started seeing each other again and the same thing happened. We had wonderful times. We had awful times. There was so much emotional conflict; and fights that should have been fought, weren't. I finally said, 'Make up your mind! I don't want to waste any more time. I'm 37 years old. I want to settle down and get married.'

She wanted to end it. I felt fine about her decision and went off to do a story on Vietnam. When I returned, she called and we had this reunion filled with wild abandon. But Charlotte still wanted to date other people. It was too crazy; I didn't want to get tempted back in, not like that. A few weeks later she met someone; two months later they were married. It was quite a blow. I'm still coming to grips with that.

So when I say I want to get married, I am very distrustful of my motives *right now*. I'm on the rebound. My current relationship best illustrates my psychological state: I am having an affair with a girl who has a boyfriend. She travels and tells her boyfriend she's coming back on a Saturday when she really returns Friday to be with me. It's not what you would call a well-rounded relationship, but it is helping me get away from the ghosts of my recent past.

That's why I'm planning where I want to be *five* years from today; I want to be living on Cape Cod with a beautiful, mature woman, a couple of kids, and a lucrative book contract! I have started to position myself professionally so that I can live any-where. Hopefully I'll meet the right woman soon—one who wants children as much as I do.

I'm not going to slip into a relationship like I had with Flavia. We went out off and on for three years before Charlotte. She was always there, someone to sleep with and take to dinner on Saturday nights. She got pregnant and I remember the days before the abortion, waking up in the middle of the night, looking over at her. I wanted to have a child, but not with Flavia.

I'm ready to have kids and I want to have them soon. I make a reasonable enough salary and have no doubts about my ability to earn money. My professional life was so disjointed up until my early 30s that never in that whole period was I ready to get married. I was on the road all the time, living in hotels, waiting in airport lounges. It's an exciting way to live, but hell on relationships—forever being uprooted. In the brief periods when I wasn't roaming around, I was chained to my computer. Sometimes I'd venture out, meet someone, get involved. But most relationships weren't sustainable. Charlotte and Flavia were my only long relationships with a bunch of little odds and ends tossed in. None led to marriage.

I think about the kind of woman I'd like to marry. Maybe someone who has a career complementary to mine is an answer. One woman I know is a camera operator. We have this joint fantasy of flying around the world making videos. Another woman I dated was a journalist. We talked about how much fun it would be to go places and do stories together. So, a woman with whom I could work to build a marriage around family and hearth would be extremely satisfying—but probably not very realistic. As anyone will tell you, marriages between people in my business usually don't last because you're traveling all the time, usually not with each other. I can even picture myself as a house husband, working from home on Cape Cod, of course, taking care of the kids. Now, to find that beautiful, mature woman who has or wants to have a child. **"**

CODY SMITH

Forty-one-year-old Cody is five feet eight inches tall and wears his reddish brown hair cut short, with an odd strand that dangles down his back. He started playing in a band when he was 18, touring Holland, Switzerland, and Belgium, where his band made hit records. But after graduating from the Juilliard School of Music, he left the performing arts to investigate other options: owning a record store, working as a part-time disc jockey, managing a women's clothing store. In 1980, he returned to music as a composer.

Cody is good-natured, friendly, and rarely bored. He has different projects going on simultaneously, sometimes working eighteen-hour days. For relaxation, he spends quiet evenings at home watching his favorite horror movies, like Nosferatu, the 1920's silent film classic.

Cody's parents have been married fifty years; he is the oldest of their seven children and has recently remarried.

Cody's Clock...

❝ I've been divorced once and lived with six different women before I married again twenty years later. Whenever there was a discussion about marriage, it centered on children, or the idea of having them.

I won't go into detail about each woman, but I was incredibly young when I married the first time. I had a nice career, thank you very much, playing in bands all over Europe. She was a very wealthy model, six years older, from the Slavic aristocracy; I was this little kid from Dover, Delaware. I thought, 'Oh my God! She wants to marry *me*!' It was all so amazing. I felt my life was charmed. 'Let's do it!'

I thought you married for life, had kids, did everything together, worked toward a common goal, and went zoom into the future. The whole marriage was very elegant but we were so completely wrong for each other. Nothing could have been a worse mistake; jumping into the jaws of an alligator might have been safer. We were married, lived together for about a year, but didn't get a divorce until four years later because she had a problem with immigration.

You know, the idea of raising a kid is really like, cool to me. I've traveled everywhere, lived everywhere, done all kinds of stuff. When I started to look around I noticed one of my friends a year younger had a daughter in her second year of college. I panicked: 'Do you want to bounce baby on your knee when you're *56* years old? The sleep deprivation, the whole thing...Better get a move on. Hey, I'm pushing the envelope already at my age. I have to act fast.'

I met Marcia at a party, but she wouldn't go out alone with me for two years. She was an attractive, bright woman who knew exactly who she was and wasn't afraid of the world or anything. She had friends in the music business who told me she didn't understand my relationship with this one particular man I had done some work for. My friends tried to tell her I was okay and gave me all sorts of opportunities: 'Hey, let's go out to dinner, Marcia can come.'

We were at a christening when I cornered her at the reception afterward. I needed to explain my position. Hell, I didn't like the guy either; he's a real S.O.B. I also knew my friends had been saying good things about me. She gave me her work number; I called about five or six times before she rang back. She was still a little hesitant, but agreed to go out with me anyway and had a great time!

We were dating regularly, taking everything in stages. I gave up my apartment downtown, moved into her place, and we began thinking about a house. Before I moved in, we talked about what was next, 'If this lasts a year we'll discuss having a baby.' She said, 'I can't have kids unless we're married. We can live together. We can do whatever you want but I just can't have a child out of wedlock. It would break my father's heart.'

Out of wedlock, those words echo in my mind. Marcia is from this stodgy Calvinistic background. For many years she had a live-in relationship. They had property together: an apartment and a house in the country. Her father would not come to either place. He didn't admonish them, he didn't act upset or angry. He simply refused to visit; it was against his morals. Her mother would stay the night, but not him. He couldn't be under the same roof as his daughter who was sleeping with a man she wasn't married to.

So we had these conversations. We talked about marriage for about a year. Marcia was 39 and hadn't had any children, so it was time. If she were 35 it might not have happened, you know, her father might have passed away so it wouldn't have been an issue. Just kidding. Knock wood that he's all right. But he does have a bad heart and the idea of freaking him out...

Anyway, we got married this year with the expectation of having a child. It's a very advantageous time for us, especially as Marcia is at the tail end of her career. She's worked for fourteen years and now her industry is being devoured by takeovers. It's like what happened to the blacksmiths—a large corporation can pay a roomful of people $20,000 for what she does. It's time to get out. Take a career break. She wants to stay home for a period of time or at least until the child is in preschool.

We talk about the money issue. What to do when Marcia is on downtime, not that looking after a child isn't work. I have several businesses and some could become serious breadwinners with a little attention. She could run them in time. I know she has the common sense to figure out whatever she wants to do. But you know, I see a very tiny percent of people getting richer and richer and everybody else slipping between the cracks. I don't want to be one of those people nor do I want my kids to fall into that bottomless pit. There isn't going to be any social security when I'm 65, so we're saving and investing, trying to protect what we have.

Making the decision to have children, and staying on a stable course is tough in today's world. These little innocent things, they don't ask to be born; you're the ones giving them life. I think all you can do is help them and nurture them and try not to screw them up. I look forward to enjoying our time together, sharing so much of what Marcia and I have learned with the children or child, if we have only one. This kid is going to become an integral part of our lives. I love kids! And can't wait to have one. I really hope this baby becomes a reality soon. God knows, we're trying. **"**

JACKSON LESLIE

Forty-eight-year-old Jackson has recently put on weight and grown a beard. Next he'll be smoking a pipe. This director of a Fortune 500 company's data processing division lives a life different from the one imagined by the Mississippi teenager who was chased out of town for filing a lawsuit against the police department. He moved to Chicago and while working in the Civil Rights Movement, obtained his first degree. Then came a masters in social work.

Jackson has mellowed some. He gave up drinking and doesn't get into heated discussions deep into the night the way he used to, yet he still plays a mean hand of poker, reads incessantly, and runs his local community group. He's kind and gentle, a man to be counted on.

Jackson's mother married when he was a child. He is the oldest of her three children and married.

Jackson's Ideal...

❝ If you're going to bring another human being into the world, you ought to be married. It cuts out a lot of grief for the child. It makes me angry when men father children, then walk away. I don't mean people should stay in bad marriages for the kids, but having children is something not to be taken lightly. I've seen children without a father who sure could have used one. Maybe I am talking about myself. I don't know, but when I was growing up, if you didn't have two parents kids laughed at you. I remember a family who lived up the street and the kids didn't have a father. It was damn hard and the other kids were so cruel. No child should have to go through that.

I got married this time to have children. Lynn and I lived together for seven years before we got married. We met at work. She was on the research side and I developed programs for her. I was at the end of a marriage; she was engaged to a serviceman. We met after work at a bar I used to frequent. If you'd seen our relationship from the start, you'd have said, 'Jesus Christ, what are those two doing together?' She didn't drink and when she did, she'd make a fool of herself. She almost got me arrested a few times. We were the odd couple and are to this day. She was this kid from Brooklyn who had never been around anyone like me. We just kept gravitating toward each other.

Eventually we bought a condominium together, co-mingled our bank accounts, shared everything. We vacationed together and didn't see other people, but marriage was out of the question because her father kept urging her to get rid of me. Holidays were hard because she wanted to see him and I wasn't welcome at the house. For a long time I told her it was okay, to go ahead, but it was pissing me off. I asked her to come to a decision. I knew trying to make two people happy was tearing her apart. It was a very rough time for us. We broke up; I was desolate. But she came around and chose me. Once Lynn committed herself, our relationship was a lot easier.

We discussed children. I said, 'If we want them, we should get married.' We had long talks and were a little nervous about it so we probably over-planned. I was so in love with the idea of being a father, although the responsibility scared me to death. I love children and always have. My friends always thought I'd make a good father. I was probably in love with the idea of being a *good* father because mine was so horrible. Well, he was my stepfather, but the only one I ever had. I grew up with anger and abuse. You know, sometimes I was scared that I might be abusive to my child. Lynn was sort of scared too. I mean, what was it going to be like for us, this white Italian woman, this black Southerner? But she wanted to get married and found this beautiful old dress...

So the more we talked, the more we talked ourselves into a wedding. None of this was an overnight decision. The ceremony was beautiful, outside in a garden on a summer's afternoon. It was so great to have our friends and Lynn's mother there. By that time we had made our peace; her father had died a few years before so that irritant was gone. Her father's best friend gave Lynn away. He's really a good guy.

We didn't have Sophia until eight years later. She's almost two years old. The disadvantage of being my age is that I have established a life pattern. I've bought the house, the cars, and the expectation of how to raise my child—what kind of care and schooling she's going to get, et cetera. I asked Lynn if she wanted to stay home. We could live differently, we could move. I'm no longer in that, 'Goddamit, you should stay home with your child' mode. I think I used to be like that. Lynn decided to return to work when Sophia was two months old. She went through her own private hell and still does, but Lynn started working when she was 18 and I'm not so sure what staying home would have done to her. I think she's a terrific mother and I'm a good dad. I can't tell you how good it feels to be a family.**"**

Four

LIFE COMMITMENT
"I want to spend eternity together."

Yes, men commit. We hear only of elusive men who don't, but what about the ones—and there are plenty—who do? Men may appear noncommittal but are more willing than we think. I remember listening to tales of woe about men unwilling to commit and finding out later they had married—but not to the women who complained about them. They don't sound so unwilling to me.

When I asked "What does marriage mean?" life commitment came in as the fourth most popular response. And these men mean it! Those who say "It's a commitment to spend the rest of our lives together" are either married, heading in that direction, or are certain they'd marry only for that reason and not much else. They have to be sure about their decision, much like Andrew Montgomery and his fifty-year breakfast test.

Commitment is an all or nothing proposition, a *cross my heart hope to die* declaration; being semicommitted-committed doesn't cut it. Men take matrimony seriously but are cautious. It's not that they don't want to commit—but precisely because they do—that their deliberations seem to take a long time.

(Men who want to marry don't use waiting as a ploy or a delaying tactic.) A man remarried in his forties said, "A marriage license should cost $50,000, a divorce $5, so that we'd all understand the commitment made. People run in and out of marriage because they don't understand the work it takes. It's not done by magic but by the way you squeeze toothpaste from the tube or leave bubbles on the soap; it's learning how to live with another person."

Let's face it, getting married takes intestinal fortitude, for both women and men. To know yourself, to trust the other person, to see the future for what it is —unsure, not plannable, full of twists and turns—can be daunting. And there's getting through the ceremony. An artist observed, "All that for better and worse stuff. You make that commitment in front of your family, your friends, and the pillars of the community. They watch you do it. They support you, that's why they all show up! It's such a public expression of your intentions." The words of marriage vows from the Book of Common Prayer spell out the terms, "...to have and to hold from this day forward, for better for worse, for richer for poorer, in sickness and in health, to love and to cherish, till death do us part, according to God's holy ordinance; and therefore I pledge thee my troth."

One of the most solemn comments is made by a then bachelor: "It means to the grave. I found myself saying this to the woman I was going to marry. One of us will be left holding the bag; one of us will bury the other. If you're looking for a bedrock attitude, that was perhaps the truest thing I'd ever said." Especially considering "my somewhat checkered emotional past," he noted.

A newly married man confided, "Marriage means commitment. A lifelong commitment to one person that will survive and thrive through the good and the bad. I thought of it abstractly but now I mean it literally." Another visualized staying together as "Part of my Protestant background: marriage means a *life* commitment. It's at the top of my list, before profession, before career. As long as it's a two-way street."

"Marriage is a long-term responsibility, not a short-term situation," a man in sales explained. "There are people who buy and sell stocks, you know trade their own accounts. A stock goes down a point, they bail out. It goes up two points, they sell. Then there are others who look at the company and think, well, this is a good investment. It's in the right industry, has a good market share, is well run. So what if the stock goes up or down? Over time it will increase in value. That's what marriage means to me; looking at the long term."

A struggling guitar player revealed, "More and more these days, girls say they won't sleep with you without a commitment. An' it's real romantic when the two of you move in together. But I am suspicious, because down the line someone's going to get hurt. You gotta commit to marriage to make the whole thing work."

A 28-year-old bachelor told me, "I think people take marriage lightly and say to themselves, 'Hey, we'll work it out.' Then they realize how complex marriage is and it's, 'Hey, let's get divorced and do something different.' I don't want to get married with that idea; I want to get married to stay married. Marriage is a commitment to stay together; otherwise, just live together and act like you're married."

I asked what is the difference between living together and marriage. A few men think there's no difference, "just a piece of paper." The majority said marriage is decidedly *much more* of a commitment and didn't rule out cohabiting as a step toward it. Although the statistics tell us that the divorce rate is higher between couples who live together prior to marriage, these men think it's a pretty good idea. It gives them the opportunity *not* to be on their best behavior, to get down to the real basics of living. As a graphic designer said, "It means I don't have to suck in my gut all the time." Interestingly enough, 40 percent of people who live together marry each other within two years.

Now hear what Parker Moses, 25, single, Mark Galeano, 51, divorced, and Arthur Rappaport, 48, married, have to say about marriage as the ultimate commitment.

PARKER MOSES

Twenty-five-year-old Parker is six foot seven inches tall, and lanky with brown hair and hazel eyes. He attended a private academy in South Carolina before graduating from the state university with a B.S. in finance. He's a trainee with an international accounting firm and has been sent to Switzerland as part of his first-year rotation.

Parker speaks with a drawl and is quite the Southern gentlemen: polite, slightly formal, Old Worldish. He was shy and restrained at first but clearly enjoyed talking, and was careful to make sure I understood his almost pre–Civil War point of view.

Parker's parents have been married thirty-two years; he is the middle child of three children, two daughters and a son. Parker is single.

Parker's Tradition...

" I'm glad I'm not in South Carolina now because everyone my age is married and it would be hard on me. My older sister was married at my age; her husband is three years older. I don't think I could marry as early as he did. There are so many things I'd like to do before I get married, like getting my career well under way so I can manage my career and my marriage. That's pretty important. I've seen men put everything into their career but lose their wives and families. I'd rather put marriage off a bit until I make it.

I used to go out with a girl whose attitude was: meet the right person, don't worry about marriage or career stuff, just live your life. When you're ready to get married, get married— but that's not very planned, that's too casual. I view marriage as a lifetime commitment, not something you fall into. You must be willing to support one another through problems, triumphs, happiness—growing old together.

In my circle of friends and family, no one is divorced. I'm acquainted with probably two divorced people. I know what the divorce statistics are but I'm not going to be one of them. *I'm marrying for keeps.* I know people say that all the time, but they don't mean it the way I do. I want to marry once and I want that marriage to stick and I want it to be a commitment for life.

I don't know how much money I'll make; I don't feel I'm totally in control of my destiny yet, but if I work hard enough, long enough, it'll be okay. I see myself as the breadwinner, the one who brings in the money and is in charge of the finances. It's fine for women to have careers but you can't have two people with high pressure jobs. One has got to have the leeway and it's not going to be me. When it comes down to it, somebody has to miss work because of family. I'll tell you when the school called to say I was sick, Mother picked me up. That's the kind of environment I was raised in.

When I was in college I dated a girl whose father asked me about my career plans, not immediately, but after we sat next to each other at a few football games. I never did answer, but he definitely implied setting me up with his company. My first reaction was, 'I'm not going to depend on a prospective father-in-law for a job!' I like the idea of saying I got where I am using my own resources. You can't let your wife's family lay out your life.

I've known enough women to know the qualities I want. The first and most important is a woman who is there for the long run, whom I can depend on forever and shares my values about religion, honesty, integrity. The South is very much a gentlemen's society—in a way, sexist. It's a place where your word is your name, and a man stands by his, and a woman stands by her man.

I picture marrying a woman from the same culture. It sounds corny but the ability to entertain is part of that way of life. I'd like a woman to enjoy throwing a dinner party, making people feel welcome, having a little tidbit to say to everyone as well as listening to what they have to impart. I'm at the age when I go out for a few brews; however, when I'm older and more established, inviting friends to the house should be a normal part of my married life.

I don't really see myself marrying a girl I've slept with before. I'm not big on someone with sexual experience. It's kind of a pet hate. I don't want to find myself at work or a party surrounded by her former lovers. She doesn't have to be a virgin but I'd rather she wasn't thought of as some loose thing, and she should be good-looking—because physical attraction is what keeps you from cheating. I know I have old-fashioned attitudes but marriage is somewhat old-fashioned. I mean the concept of being married to one person your whole life really slipped away the generation before mine. What a shame.

I'm explaining very much a conservative Southerner's position. I debated issues like racism, homosexual rights, and the death penalty with a Yankee girlfriend of mine once. I ran into a wall, not being able to get around my predispositions, and had to reconsider where I stood. That experience had quite an effect on me. I think everyone should keep up on current events and have an intellectual perspective, so I'd look for that in a wife as well.

I have this image of my putting off marriage until I'm in my 40s, then marrying a beautiful 23-year-old right out of college who's looking for someone secure. Pretty horrible? And not very realistic. I have memories of asking a girl out and her turning me down for a guy five years older, who drove a BMW and already had a career.

Frankly, I don't think that would be too hard to do. In my senior year in college, lots of my classmates panicked if they didn't have a career or a boyfriend. Certainly it wasn't the majority of girls, but those sorority types don't want careers; they see themselves devoting time to the Junior League or the local community organization. I know it can't happen. I'm too young and I'm working too hard to even consider dating anyone, let alone start courting, that's pretty formal. But it sure is fun to daydream about while I'm sweating over a hot balance sheet.**"**

MARK GALEANO

Fifty-one-year-old Mark is at least six feet tall, with dark eyes and black hair. After graduating from high school and being honorably discharged from the Marine Corps, he started several businesses in the New York metropolitan area; the latest, a small products development company, has proven to be one of his most successful.

Mark is one snappy dresser: bow ties, white shirts with French cuffs, shoes adorned with tassels. He has a confidence about him that easily could harden into arrogance—but hasn't, as far as I can tell. He's outgoing, charming, and warm.

His mother is a widow; he's the youngest of fifteen children, six daughters and nine sons. Mark is divorced and has two children in their 20s.

Mark's Quest...

❝ I grew up in the Italian part of Brooklyn; my parents are of Neapolitan descent. When I was 16, a new family with a 15-year-old daughter moved next door to my aunt and uncle, a block away. Liana was pretty, Neapolitan, and got to know my family. How could I go wrong? I'm going back a-ways when marrying the same nationality was *very* important.

After high school, I joined the Marines and when I got out, my next responsibility was to get married. Liana's father passed on so I felt even more obligated. That was the value system: you marry, have children, get a job that puts food on the table. Once accomplished, these tasks made you a mature adult. So a year later we married, and by the time I was 25 had two children. Very clearly I didn't know any better and had gone along with some tribal custom.

My relationship with Liana had always been tumultuous. However, I had an illusion about marriage: When I was a kid I broke my arm; the doctor put a cast on it, so I thought the pain would stop, and I remember being shocked when it still hurt. To me that marriage was like putting on a cast; I thought it would make us okay, but it didn't.

We almost broke up right away but I managed to hold the marriage together for eight years because of my kids. It was very important to have a relationship with my children and especially to keep a strong connection with my son because I didn't have any with my father. All he did was get up in the morning, go to work, walk home a couple of miles—so as not to spend money on public transportation—eat his pasta, drink his wine, and fall asleep in his chair before going to bed. There wasn't much money or communication. The longest conversation I had with my father lasted maybe four minutes, although he lived until I was in my 30s. There was no talk of sex and certainly never any discussion about whether I should or should not marry. Even my older brother stood by while I, this schmucky kid, walked down the aisle. He must've had some idea since he didn't marry until well into his 30s, but said nothing.

After my divorce I continued to build up my various businesses and had a second childhood enjoying the bachelor life. For twenty years I had countless chances to satisfy any physical or psychological need. I was in and out of relationships, lived with four different women; it was fun. All I really needed was the strength, the time, and the money.

I am considered pretty okay: fairly successful, well-traveled, living on the East side in my own brownstone with a garden. Friends say, 'We have someone for you, we don't want to push, *but* you're absolutely made for each other.' They roll out her qualities: she loves cooking or gardening or she's a big earner. It's fairly constant.

A few years ago it all got a little stale, I was in that Peggy Lee 'Is That All There Is?' mode. I didn't want to spend my life constantly on the make. I cohabited, my life intertwined with whomever, but I wasn't psychologically committed. There were sparks but when push came to shove, I'd pass. I was with a woman more for convenience than for wanting, *really* wanting to be with her, or so I thought. But it really went back to not trusting myself or women. I wasn't sure about myself or what I was feeling, so I rejected it all. I really didn't think a loving and committed relationship was obtainable because my experiences with women hadn't been good from the beginning. I didn't have a good relationship with my mother, my sisters, or my ex-wife.

So l started to do some more work to get in touch with the hidden parts of myself. I've always been a searcher and had overcome other blocks before, such as my fear of success. I studied and practiced different philosophies, trying to release negative feelings, and went to spiritual workshops, spending weekends at retreats to do the internal digging. I peeled away layer after layer and felt more vulnerable, and at the same time found a feminine aspect within myself. I started to feel more comfortable revealing *myself* to women instead of only my physical parts.

While I was going to all these workshops I met Suzanne, who was enchanting and initially prepared to commit. After six months of living together I realized we were looking for different things. I wanted a commitment and she didn't. It's now obvious that I need to 'put out there' the type of woman I want for a partner and when she comes along, I'll marry her.

Besides wanting a woman ready for a commitment, I hope she'll be connected to spirituality somehow and be willing to show her feelings and love. Maybe she'll like being in the country, puttering around, arranging flowers. I like tall, attractive, square-shouldered women, outdoor rugged types who help unload the car and who won't take any shit.

I hope that when I find this woman she'll understand that a commitment is not only to each other but to the third thing— our marriage. People tell me you have to 'work' at a relationship; I never liked that term but now I understand marriage has to be a work in progress. You both have to step back and look at it. You can't always keep everything sweet and wonderful—so what if everything isn't running smoothly? If you can't talk about a problem it won't just disappear: it returns to bite you in the ass.

Couples must set aside a moment to discuss where their lives are moving and what their feelings are. If little things don't feel right, take the opportunity to share them before they grow bigger and uglier and bunch up together, so you can't separate them out. Also, if you don't spend part of your time searching inside yourself, complacency sets in and the ground can shift beneath you. You've got to keep working at it, and that's another part of the commitment I plan to make. **"**

ARTHUR RAPPAPORT

Forty-nine-year-old Art is six feet eight inches tall, weighs 315 pounds, with brown hair and eyes. While playing for the New York Giants he commuted to Georgetown, getting an MBA and credits toward a Ph.D. He's a regional sales manager for a Dutch company, and lives in Houston.

Art had a heart transplant there two years ago; his doctors counted the days waiting for a major holiday like Labor Day to roll around. People killed in car accidents are a good source for hearts. "A macabre reality sets in when you're down to your last two weeks with a bad ticker," he told me ruefully.

Art's parents were married forty-seven years; his father, a widower, recently remarried. Art is the eldest of five sons and he has an older sister. Art is married, with an 11-year-old son.

Art's Story...

❝ I didn't marry until I was 36. My mother had given up hope! I was always on the move, traveled all over—Chicago, Atlanta, Kansas City—and was really part of the singles scene. While I lived in Washington I joined the Junior Officers and Professional Men's Association. You bought a membership and there was a cash bar. I must have met hundreds of women that way—the founder rounded up every good-looking woman in town. He later went on to start Club Med.

If a woman could talk, she would interest me. I talk for a living. A woman who could carry on a conversation had the potential for being a date or a friend; she didn't have to have boobs out to her elbows. I like a woman who sparkles, and taller women, because I'm so big. I usually scare women. I know in the back of her mind she thinks, 'What will he do to me when we're alone?' She'd have to think I was safe, that I wasn't going to hurt her.

When I asked a woman for her telephone number, I really wanted to see her: no BS, no test, no graduation procedure. But I had to feel she was comfortable with me, that helped me feel comfortable with her. If I liked her enough, I hoped she would reciprocate the feeling. But, you know, women are cold in terms of their selection process. Pick up any singles newspaper— they're all looking for a man six-foot-two, with blue eyes and muscles, having a good hair day. Women think men are difficult! Not every man looks like Tom Selleck; some are bald, some are Teutonic, or some are Mediterranean. You stand us all up naked and we all have the same basic equipment but not everyone has perfect teeth. What's wrong with a little compromise?

Friends introduced me to Laura. She was just getting out of a pretty horrendous second marriage and was a widow before that. We are quite a pair visually. I remember we went to the movies once and I overheard the woman behind the popcorn counter say, 'There goes King Kong and Twiggy.' We thought it was doubly funny, because Laura was a model at one time.

Laura and I lived together in her apartment for six or seven months before we got married. It was a good tune up. Living together increases your chances of being compatible. After the newness wears off, you walk around in your underwear, let your defenses, your guard, down. And if the affection is still there— you take the next step. I signed on for the future.

Marriage means finding someone to spend the rest of your life with, to have children with, to vacation with, to die with. My parents were married for forty-seven years and had a good marriage; all of their children were well raised, all went to college, all are successful. My objective is to be as happy as they were. I'm aware that they had some strife but overcame it. My view is that you marry, pitch in, there are tough times but you weather it. No one in my family on either side has been divorced, until my younger brother recently.

I figured when I asked Laura to marry me, we'd stay married. I didn't approach marriage lightly. You have a 50:50 chance but I *never* considered that 50:50 chance. I have friends that are 0-for-2, 0-for-3—yet I made the assumption that my marriage would last.

We have been married for thirteen good years. The last two have been hard on Laura. We didn't know I had a heart problem until my first heart attack and believe me, it's the rare individual who can handle all the problems endemic to a heart transplant patient. I get grouchy because I can't eat the foods I like, can't drink, sometimes can't sleep. I could end up in a wheelchair or on life support. The average life expectancy of a transplant patient is five years, but I hope to beat those statistics and live until I'm 65. It's too soon to leave my wife and son alone.**"**

Five

TRUST
"It's a must."

Would you marry someone you couldn't trust? It's such an obvious ingredient in any marriage. Yet for many men, trust is the primary reason for slicing through layers of wedding cake. They want a woman they can count on and make a big point of emphasizing loyalty and honesty. They lament giving their hearts to women who throw them over, who broadcast their secrets, who make jokes at their expense. Divorced men especially talk about ex-wives changing the rules and going back on agreements once the mortgage is approved and signed. They refuse to believe these permutations are part of the ebb and flow of marriage, viewing them instead as a form of betrayal.

Over the years a sixth sense develops. A man in his late 40s told me, "I've dated so many women I can see behind the facade; they become transparent. Especially those with hidden agendas and ones who try to second guess me—like pretending to be crazy about what I like—instead of being themselves. An article in *Cosmopolitan* says men like dogs, so they buy a cocker spaniel. I know men play games too; we masquerade as dentists or doctors because we think that's what women want. I understand desperation—but it's not honest." He continued, "Giving mixed signals is an early sign; that clear contrast between body language and words. If a woman walks in wearing a low-cut dress, and tells you about the years she spent in Calcutta with Mother Theresa, something is *definitely* wrong."

One man watched the woman he'd been living with for six months mutate before his very eyes. "I thought she was strong, self-sufficient, fun. We were going to get married until she turned into a nagging harpy—really weird. All of a sudden it was '*We've* got to do this, *we've* got to do that.' Even her values changed; she became totally obsessed with money. Buzzers and bells went off in my head. I mean she was being one person to get one thing and once she got it, another person emerged. Sorta like a butterfly turning into a worm. It was like a horror film."

A newlywed in his 30s said, "You have to really get to know the person, and find out as much as is humanly possible, before you get married. Make sure you have an honest relationship. I guess there are some things you don't have to tell your spouse; you have your own life to lead, but to purposely hide things is pretty bad."

Trust is fragile. Men gave examples of their loved one's secret lives. Once the truth was uncovered, their relationships were never quite the same, and some soured, like Barry's, whose second marriage broke up six months ago. "It is most important both sides be honest. I'd been married five years before I was aware my ex-wife waited until I was asleep to race to the 7 Eleven for fig newtons! I was flabbergasted. Here was a whole side of my ex-wife I knew nothing about, and her closet eating had gone on *five* years. You know, I wondered why she continually asked me whether I'd still love her if she got fat..." He's already started to question his latest flame, almost in a desperate need to know if she plans any cover-up.

A father of three warned, "I think telling lies is a risky business. I can recall someone I cared for going to Paris with women friends. After a week I called her hotel; she wasn't registered. I called the *other* fourteen in the hotel chain; she was in none of them. Upon her return, she told me they stayed with some guys they'd met the previous summer in Greece. It was a big blow. She said nothing happened, but that wasn't the point. She never intended to stay in a hotel—not too conducive of trust."

Men look for signs early in a relationship. A grad student told of not calling back a date: "Carla wasn't a trusting person. She asked if she could leave her jewelry in my apartment the day we went for a bike ride. But first, she had to make sure none of my friends had a key—she was afraid they'd come in and steal her bracelets. I didn't confront her as much as I should have, but after she left, it bothered me. I mean, who thinks like that?"

There can be no love, no commitment, no future together without trust. Meet four men, each of whom wouldn't touch a woman with a ten-foot pole unless she passed his test: Harry Lamaire, 51, Lee Weston, 46, Thomas Duke, 37, and Jack Evans, 29.

HARRY LAMAIRE

Fifty-one-year-old Harry is tall, attractive with a thin face, steel blue eyes, dark brown hair. He looks just as polished in running sweats as he does in suits from Ralph Lauren. Harry didn't stay long at college in New Hampshire, preferring the active world of broadcasting to the torpor of the classroom. Self-educated, he often grabs any opportunity to show off his knowledge, especially of history, which is considerable.

Harry's life turns on a schedule that's difficult by any measure, rising to prepare for his on-air performance long before most night owls consider turning in, and working weekends. He maintains a supremely professional demeanor: unhurried, warm, and relaxed, but you know the pressure must get to him.

Harry's father and older brother are both dead. His mother did not remarry. Harry is married for the third time, and has two stepchildren and a baby daughter.

Harry's Discovery...

❝ You can't be proud of two divorces. Those were really spectacular mistakes and I'm not proud of them. But in those years, my 20s and 30s, the last thing I could ever admit was having been party to failure. So I was a finger pointer. If she had been this and hadn't been that...It didn't occur to me until well into my 40s to consider that I played a rather large role in those failures.

As a youngster I had the unfortunate tragic circumstance of the death of my mother's husband, my dad, my brother's father. He basically left overnight: he had a heart attack and went. I was eight; my brother was 15. And I am sure that any number of people would feel the same way—nothing is ever certain again. If your whole world can be turned upside down in a night, what have you to count on?

And maybe that explains the way I lived for the longest time, as if it were, how would you say, evanescent. Life is such a hazardous proposition and there's a real risk in the way you perceive it. I didn't take anything seriously, didn't invest much emotionally; other than the career nothing else was important. If it came down to a question of a relationship or pursuing the snark of a career, the snark would win every time.*

The snark I knew. The snark I could count on. After some career reversal, I remember my first wife saying, 'Well, that's the end of you.' And I heard myself saying, 'No, dear, that's the end of you.' The divorce didn't occur that moment. Believe me, it was long, painful, and expensive, but that was the moment I turned my back on that marriage. Even if I didn't know what a proper definition of marriage was, I knew there was something dreadfully wrong about a wife who could take a job reversal and state it in those terms.

*A snark is an imaginary animal created by Lewis Carroll in his poem "The Hunting of the Snark," (1876). It represents dreams and goals.

In marriage the single most important ingredient is trust—in oneself, in the entity the two of you have created. Absent trust, you have nothing. In time trust should build up in any relationship.

I once said to a woman with whom I was involved, 'If I can't trust you what have we got?' And I didn't know how firm was the ground I stood on in those days. She said I was a controlling bastard. Ah, perhaps she was right!

I don't think you can have good sex without trust. To revel in who you are, to let go and have the kind of sex that helps you get through is impossible without trust. All the fantasy, everything displaced from work and dealings with other people is brought to bed. Sex with a trusted partner is the best you can feel on this planet; everyone is looking for that kind of release, that kind of pleasure. That's why there are drugs.

But how can you ask anyone to relinquish that much control to have a really—call it a cosmic orgasm or a splendid sexual life—if they don't trust you? It's a very vulnerable spot for men and women, putting your life in someone else's hands. I'm afraid it's difficult on a one night stand basis; a lot of what passed for sex in my life could be called internal masturbation. You don't know that until you know the difference, until it *is* different, vastly different, like night and day. It's the quality of the release for those seconds you are totally in the care of the person you love. It's so difficult to achieve because it's so hard to trust.

I've been in relationships where things that had given pleasure in the past became threatening. My partner said, 'Don't do that anymore. I never really liked that.' Months before it had been something we prized doing together—from taking a shower together to revealing part of our sexual nature. When those pleasures are withdrawn, and either party is apt to withdraw them over a longish relationship, then something is wrong. There's no trust because those things should be enlarged upon, not diminished.

I started up with my second wife while I was still married to my first because she looked pretty good in comparison. Looking back that's what I usually did. One relationship would segue into the other, so I didn't have time to think. I had a prior requirement to keep myself from being alone.

After my second divorce I lived with a woman for six years. She said, 'Skip me, marry the next one.' I must have looked terrible to her. One wounded bird picks another I guess. Emotionally I couldn't tie my shoe laces and I wasn't paying attention to anything other than the career pursuit. But I left her and by then I had someone else! Isn't that awful?

At the end of that relationship, which was explosive—full of endless separations and reconciliations—I asked myself, 'How many failures do you need?' There had to be a way to break the cycle. I used to say my emotional life was like a football game, an endless series of 52–0 Saturdays. When I thought I could get deep with a woman, I usually would meet a wall of resistance; on the other hand, when I was presented with a woman who could be deep, then *my* resistance would go up.

For two years I didn't do anything of a permanent nature and those were very significant years. I dated. There was a progression of women but no one moved in and I didn't marry anyone! And slowly I began to take stock of the mess that was my life— two marriages, two live-ins, four principal relationships—and decided to follow the suggestion of a dear friend. I sought, as they say, professional help.

Meanwhile, I had lunch with a charming woman I had met through work. Her name is Alex. We sat down at 2:30 in the afternoon and finished at 10:30 that evening. We sat at the table and simply talked as if we had known one another for years. It was the first time we'd been alone together and we spent it in a public place for eight hours. I liked her so. I remember thinking, this is not an ordinary person. Based on that I proceeded more carefully. It was a matter of taking it seriously at one degree or the other.

From that day forward I decided there would be no suggestion of anything even mildly dishonest or disloyal. Who was I being disloyal to? Me. I was sure I wasn't going to do anything to give her the slightest moment's doubt. She knew I had quite a reputation and later told me I didn't look like a man who could be depended upon. Perhaps that meeting was the catalyst for change—a possibility of something more, of something good. I hoped. Hope is powerful. I remember an older friend who met Alex cautioning, 'At last, a functioning woman, and a worthy opponent. Try not to screw it up!'

While we were getting to know each other, I asked Alex gently about her emotional life. I knew she was at the end of a marriage but she told me there was someone else in the picture. A few months later we stuck a bargain, Alex agreed to 'divorce' *both* men and I called off some relationships that were extant, simply saying good-bye.

On paper, our getting married looked like a mountain of difficulty: Alex had two small children, needed to get a divorce, and sell her house; I was a bachelor with two marriages behind him, living in a small apartment. The financial arena in which we found ourselves was suddenly larger than I'd ever been in, but this outwardly problematical relationship turned out to be the least troublesome.

Had I had any insight, all the good things that have happened since I met Alex *might* have happened earlier. I'm not so sure I really bought that I was a worthless, controlling son of a bitch. I always thought I could be faithful, I always thought I could be a good husband, and once in awhile I dared to hope I could be a good parent. But there was so much turmoil ahead of those potential successes.

Alex made me confront those issues. We worked on trust. You know, life is a very real and terrible thing to contemplate, but now I believe there is joy. Joy in caring for someone and being cared for, in watching the children grow and learn, joy in a relationship you can trust. I think we'll be able to withstand the worst and enjoy the best.**"**

LEE WESTON

Forty-six-year-old Lee is dark eyed, powerfully built, and exhibits a blend of animal magnetism and earnestness. He grew up in a show business family, and obtained a bachelor of arts in drama and Latin before setting out to become an actor/producer in Los Angeles and New York.

Lee is very personable and chatty, but not easy to get a fix on. I got the feeling he doesn't ask much from people, that he sits back and watches, letting them come to him. He's a loner in a very gregarious business. Lee told me, "I tend to live in my own world. Someone called it Leeville or Leetown or something like that. I'm in my head a lot. At times, 'It's earth to Lee, earth to Lee.'"

Lee's parents were married forty-eight years. His father died recently. Lee has a younger brother and sister. He's single.

Lee's Quandary...

❝ In the mid-'70s I became deeply involved with Julie. I was capti-
vated. She was this bright, open, happy woman with incredible
spirit, newly separated from her husband. She was really into
freedom for women, especially sexual freedom, which was damn
difficult for me since our sex life was so wonderful. I had this
totally abandoned feeling—loving Julie and getting the physical
stuff. I've had good sex since but I've not been able to put the two
together. I don't think I've *really* been in love since Julie.

We lived in different towns and she took advantage of it by
sleeping with other guys. She said it was meaningless, that she
loved me but was just lonely. Not that she slept with that many,
maybe two, but it upset me so. She didn't seem to understand
the delicate stage we were in—building trust and respect. She
was going to kill this thing. I told her it was like planting a garden and then stomping all over it with jack boots. Those little
seedlings weren't going to spring back. We had all these arguments; maybe I could have found a way to come to terms with
her behavior, but I lost trust in her.

Much later Julie admitted it was partly her fault we broke up.
I still have this image: we're standing face to face, wearing gun
belts. Neither one of us is willing to drop our guns. You know,
take the gun out of your holster, throw it on the floor, now the
other one. I knew if either of us dropped our guns, the other
would shoot.

Can you tell trust is a *big* issue for me? Very often I err on
the side of almost childlike women now. I guess it is because I
need to see their pain, some of their vulnerability, to feel comfortable. I'm not so sure it makes them more trustworthy but it
certainly makes me feel less threatened.

I'm a strange bird, never having been married at 46. I wish I
could answer, 'Yeah, I've been married a couple of times.' Then

all those who ask me might think to themselves, 'Whew, he's fine. He's straight. Or he's not a psychotic.'

But you know, I *never* saw myself as one of those guys who'd marry at 24 or 25 to raise a family. Never being that conventional, I knew I'd marry late. But I've gotten further along than I thought without taking a crack at it. I fantasized about hearing thunder, I'd fall for a woman, and proclaim to the world at large, 'I can't help myself, I gotta get married!' I'm beginning to worry that it *really* is a fantasy. Pretty soon I'll be able to have a woman like that genetically engineered.

I think I am afraid of getting married, afraid I'd botch it. I also don't choose the right candidates. The women I spend time with could never work for me in the long run, given what I want and look for. I probably intentionally seek them out. And there is nothing I hate more than endings and believe me, I've seen a few. Add in the legal system, the friends, both families—it's a nightmare.

I thought my best friend had a wonderful marriage. He got married at 32 to a terrific woman, supportive and loving. They bought a house, had a kid, really seemed to care about each other. Fourteen years later it turned to shit. I was caught in the middle when we were driving to a party. The whole way in the car, George's wife said awful things to him. He'd tell a story or make a comment and she'd put him down, sneer at him, 'Yeah, what do *you* know?' I wanted to hang her from the nearest tree! He finally walked out, she became so nasty. I'm not saying George was blameless; he's opinionated, works twelve hour days and must have done plenty to piss her off. Their divorce was an ugly, twisted mess.

You know, I'm terrible at meeting women. I spend a lot of time alone. I don't 'date,' well, hardly ever. I'm not like so many men in my profession. When I get along with a woman I have a tendency to go out *only* with her. I am not one of those guys who thumbs through his little black book scheduling Lisa for

Wednesday, Marianne for Saturday night. I don't live my life like that.

Friends are always fixing me up. The last woman I split up with, I was introduced to through a friend at his Christmas party. Everybody started to dance so he shoved me toward her. I would have never met her on my own—she was a little young. One woman I went out with for awhile I sat next to at an Al-Anon meeting; another I met on the tennis courts. I am quite flattered when women decide to get involved with me, but I get so comfortable that I let relationships go too far. Inevitably the topic of marriage comes up, and I'm cast as the failure because I don't want to marry them. I'm the bad guy: Mr. Noncommitment. It's painful for those women but painful for me in a different way. I know I'm idealistic, still looking for something so completely right that I'm swept away by a 'gotta be with you' feeling.

I'm too judgmental; I don't like that about myself. I rule women out quickly and have probably missed some wonderful women but I can tell—within minutes—if there is any potential for a long-term relationship, a friendship, or if she's someone I'd just like to have a few laughs with. I see the negatives immediately; I can't abide a woman who only worries about her manicure and wardrobe—that shop 'til you drop mentality is a deal breaker and candy box perfect blondes don't interest me. I prefer dark, exotic looks. Nor do I go for women looking to me for answers; I eventually lose respect for their lack of independence.

I'd like a woman who genuinely likes men. A woman who grew up with brothers usually understands and likes men more. I was once prompted by a professional with an M.D. to make a list! A woman who is gentle, supportive, has a sense of humor, one who is fairly happy, and thinks I'm an addition to her life—not the only reason she exists—is what I'm looking for.

I keep going back to this trust issue; manipulation is part of it. Women's magazines and literature are ripe with the notion women have to snare a man, hook a man, dress for a man. This 'he's going to like me better if I do this' approach. That turns me off big time. It's not to say that I don't respond when my lady wears a certain dress. But if she has a *system*—today she puts on the dress, tomorrow she cooks my favorite food, the next day she's dying to ride my Harley—it's duplicitous. This can include sex, incidentally, all aimed at getting me to marry her. The dress changes, so does the food and the fake enthusiasm. What's left? It's more than a question of *just* getting married; her actions have to be genuine. If they aren't, nothing else will work, and I see a price tag hanging there, blowing in the breeze.

I'm *trying* to give up my old ways, I don't go out with fixer-uppers anymore (you know, a little wiring here, new baseboards there), the childlike women, the neurotics. I'm wising up. I look for women who are healthier, less troubled. The young one I met at the Christmas party was a step in the right direction; she worked hard but managed to have a well-rounded life. She is a very stable personality in a very unstable business and I'm a little envious of her for that.

I'm getting closer. Maybe the right relationship would give me a reason to settle in one place; on the other hand, settling in one place might lead me to the right relationship! It's Catch-22. A committed relationship should be my goal. I should say it out loud—make it real instead of playing with the fantasy. It's about time I gave it a shot. **"**

THOMAS DUKE

Thirty-seven-year-old Thomas has green eyes and light brown hair, and wears button-down shirts and khaki pants. He worked his way through Amherst as a college correspondent for papers like *The Philadelphia Inquirer,* the *Los Angeles Times,* and the *Detroit Free Press,* graduating with a bachelor of arts in American history. He's a reporter for a major magazine.

Thomas loves gossip, hates exercise, and has an almost encyclopedic knowledge of current affairs, history, music, politics, and art. Setting high standards for himself and others—he works too hard and takes his obligations seriously. I found him approachable, congenial, and forthcoming.

His parents have been married forty years, and Thomas is their only child. He's single.

Thomas' Disillusionment...

❝ Gwen and I had been going together for about two years when I proposed—no, suggested (propose being a loaded word)—that we live together. Three months later Gwen gave me her answer. Here's what happened. One Sunday I got a call from the magazine telling me to get over to cover a story. (We spent most weekends together and on Sunday mornings she got up early to run.) While I was scrambling to take a shower and get dressed, Gwen came back in and announced, 'I've decided we *shouldn't* live together.' And that's all I heard. I thought it odd of her to pick that moment. Then she said something like, 'That's it, I'm outta here.' I remember my jaw falling open because that's not what I expected her to say—I assumed we'd eventually get married and my asking her to live with me was step one. Talk about a crisis situation!

Gwen maintains she said, 'I decided we shouldn't live together *unless we're getting married.*' Was I so stunned by the first half of the sentence I hadn't listened to the second half? You know, my work life depends on hearing people right—communication professional blows it! I don't think she actually completed the sentence. She must have seen my face change and backed off.

I said something like, 'Let's talk about it later.' Admittedly, had there been any time for discussion, I might have focused on what she meant and not taken her so literally. It may sound pompous but I tend to think people are as deliberate as I try to be. I had put off pressuring Gwen. I rehearsed the words in my mind so they'd come out right. I couldn't just blurt out, 'Boy, am I on pins and needles waiting for you to make up your mind.' I didn't want to risk losing the best thing that had come along.

Four weeks later we got back together and immediately started arguing. I never paid enough attention to her; I wasn't as serious as she was about our relationship. But the root cause of our disagreement was my continual 'deception.' Gwen dredged up two examples to prove her point, 'You deceived me on our first date. You said your father worked for the government.' I think there's a limit to what you tell someone on a date, especially if you may never see her again. (My father's a defense contractor.) 'You deceived your parents all along by not telling them we have a sex life.' Of course I didn't volunteer information about our sex life to my parents! They are very religious and I'm sure they knew, but they never asked, so I never had to lie.

Gwen also imagined I was fooling around with other women, probably because her previous boyfriend had two women going at the same time. Neither knew about the other until they met each other at the same party. Can you imagine? A horrible scene ensued and he dumped Gwen. I know the other woman; she even looks like Gwen. I also know the former boyfriend. (It's odd and incestuous—we'll be in therapy yet!)

I was in love with Gwen and thought everything could be smoothed out. Until her talk about deception made me lose my temper and call the whole thing off. I fumed 'I don't see how I can be in a relationship where I don't feel trusted. That's what all this has raised.'

After we broke up Gwen dropped by to retrieve her running shoes, leaving a note which put me in another snit. She wrote, 'I talked to Ann about what you're going through.' (Ann is her running partner.) I deliberately had *not* told any of my friends and there she was telling Ann, 'Thomas is having a midlife crisis at the age of 36!' Or some such. I flew off the handle: Who the heck was Ann to know anything about me? She didn't interview me and of all our friends, she knew me the least. I thought Gwen was a private enough person to keep her own counsel. It seemed really out of character and signified a major breach of trust. Then her note said, 'I hope some day *I* and my running shoes can come back.' Of course I continued in my snit, muttering to myself—and in bad grammar to boot!

Later we tried getting back together, but I felt badly burned and apparently so did Gwen. I think we both felt let down. Trust is such a basic thing that once lost, it's hard to regain. It was a problem from day one for Gwen and nothing I could do altered her perception. Nor could I imagine anything changing in the foreseeable future. So the relationship was over. Time to move on.

It's tricky because there isn't a world of female persons hanging around waiting for me, especially funny, smart ones who will roll with the punches. My schedule is erratic. I often call up and plead, 'Emergency, I can't be there. The tickets are at the box office. Get yours and I'll meet you when I can.' That kind of behavior doesn't always play well during the first stages of a relationship.

Certainly I would like to meet a woman with whom I could feel comfortable and trust enough not to betray me; nor would I knowingly betray her. To be sure that no matter what stupid things I pull, no matter what stupid things she pulls, we're not going to get so infuriated that we can't talk it out. I mean everyone acts like a clod—we forget birthdays, but if that's as bad as it gets, I'd probably be able to live with it if she would forgive me. I don't know what I'm like; I'm probably not as easy as I think. She'd have to deal with my silly nonsense, without sticking my nose in it, unless, of course, I deserved it.

I'm keeping my eyes open for appropriate women and have come across a few, but I'm a little scared about investing a lot of hope then getting tremendously disappointed for motives I can't foresee. Despite what I do for a living, being expected to be cynical and have an edge and all, I *am* trusting until given reason not to be.**"**

JACK EVANS

Twenty-six-year-old Jack is so slight that if he didn't have dark eyes and hair, he wouldn't be visible at all. He dropped out of college after two years, and worked at a series of jobs in Ohio, before making good money as a commodities trader. He's now living off his earnings while considering another career move.

His friends say Jack is a good joke teller, jazzing up stories with perfect accents and mannerisms, and has been known to burst into song. But the Jack I met was quiet, thoughtful, and wary.

Jack's parents separated but remained married until his father died a few years ago. He's an only child and single.

Jack's Caution...

❝ I'm looking for the one person I can trust in this vast sea of idiots without giving it a second thought, someone with whom I can completely let my hair down and confide feelings I tell no one else. I trust very few people. I don't want to marry and remarry: only one marriage for me.

I went through my parents' separation and I have male friends who have been married and divorced at least twice—those women and their lawyers took them to the cleaners! Although I have no reason for not wanting to marry, other than I don't have a job right now, I'm very cautious about women. Maybe I've only heard the man's side.

I've dated for ten years, and once in a while I've asked myself, 'Is this the person you want to spend the rest of your life with?' So far the answer has been 'No.' Sometimes the woman I'm seeing and I both know there's no future, but we continue going out with each other anyway. It's good not to have the pressure of constantly asking 'Where is this relationship going?' Those women are still my friends.

I don't have a steady girlfriend now but I wish I had one. I dwell on it a lot those Saturday nights I spend in front of the TV imagining couples out, doing things together. I go to bars and nightclubs, but that scene is fairly discouraging for someone my age. Women I'm interested in all go for older men with limos or foreign types with greasy hair or ponytails. The most attractive ones are arrogant and the younger ones—18, 19, 20—are bitchy. I don't know why they think they're going to be young for the rest of their lives. They should wake up. The men they spurn will have found someone else by the time they're ready; others won't give them a second glance once they pass their 25th birthdays. Interestingly enough, older women—32, 33, 34—are much easier to approach in clubs or anywhere else because they're more realistic about themselves and about what it takes to get involved. And then there are those women of any age who stay in physically or emotionally abusive relationships because they're so afraid of being alone; they'd rather have a lousy relationship than nothing. Who wants a woman with an inferiority complex?

I don't always go to bars to meet women. I've met some at work, on blind dates, at parties. My mother keeps pushing me toward her friends' daughters, some of which aren't so bad. But I'm cautious. For instance, I met a woman who worked at the frame store around the corner from my place. We just got to talking after I picked out a frame; I found her interesting and attractive, so I asked her out—or at least tried to. But every time I called her, she was busy but asked me to call again. After about ten calls we finally made a date for dinner. Obviously I had a crush on her, or I wouldn't have put myself through all that aggravation. During dinner (which was great fun) she not only told me she had a boyfriend, but that he knew where we were having dinner! The whole setup was weird. I could tell she liked me, and I certainly liked her but what the hell was she doing? Setting me up? Wasn't one boyfriend enough? I told her to call me if things changed: I put her on hold mentally.

Sure, I'd like to be in love, have a wife and a child, but I need to get settled in a job to feel secure about my own life. Then again, I'm so tired of dating I wonder if I don't view every date as a marriage prospect. We could live together for a year with an eye toward marriage. Take time to really get to know each other—there's a lot to be said for sharing a bathroom—and hopefully establish a good foundation of trust. I'd have to be careful about making the wrong decision, otherwise only her lawyers make out. **"**

Six

SHARED VALUES
"We sorta match."

Opposites attract—it's all so very intriguing in the beginning. After a while that "oppositeness" becomes opposition. What was once an endearing little discussion about soccer looses its charm after too many replays. That exotic, hot Thai restaurant dulls in comparison to the rediscovered thrill of driving under the golden arches. Differences in taste, lifestyle, and attitude rapidly become a mark against the relationship's permanence. An uneasiness begins to develop—even boredom. Small reminders of the old days crop up. The little voice says, "What am I doing here?"

Men who marry for the same values want a woman who is familiar and recognizable. A 42-year-old jokes, "Baby, if we two really have it in common, nothing else matters. We can live in a shack in Tasmania and be happy together!" But he goes on to say that if commonality *isn't* found, the differences take over, leading to "hopeless conflict."

Some similarities that may seem at first insignificant: both breaking into tears over the same movie scene, agreeing not to put the ketchup bottle on the dining room table; or as a polo player said, "Liking rice, or the color blue." They quickly transcend to issues of larger importance: having and raising children; handling finances; deciding where to live. An ambitious man admitted, "I'm driven by success, money, and power and the woman I'd marry would have to feel the same."

A 36-year-old told me, "I didn't marry the type of woman I'd been dating. They weren't warm or compassionate and didn't look at things the same way. In hindsight, I dated them because I *didn't* want to get married. Those differences automatically built a wall. When I met my wife, it struck home that we looked at the world the same way: our reactions to political events, job situations, family, are very much the same. Even when we told each other about how we acted in different situations, it was 'Yeah, that's what I would have done.' "

Parallels were highlighted by friends and family who, although different, had "known" patterns and habits. This newly married man continued, "My wife's family made me feel at home, not that they all rushed over to shake my hand, but they felt like my family. Even her friends were similar to mine. It was all so comfortable and automatic, I didn't have to work at it. Sorta like a package arriving fully assembled, I didn't have to read the instructions to figure out how it worked."

Life also is easier and more directed when a couple has the same outlook. A publisher told me, "I think people need a common goal, especially people who decide to get married, because you need to operate from the same pages of a book. The unit formed is stronger than the individual."

A 50-year-old confided, "A friend told my fiancée that it wasn't necessarily bad to have the same background, and I concur. It makes the day-to-day stuff easier and expectations aren't so different."

Men commented about differences *not* working. A Washingtonian observed, "I think you will find that people from different backgrounds don't tend to get involved. People from

Rodeo Drive aren't going to date someone from Watts. When you think about it, what do they have in common?"

A race car driver says the nation's divorce rate has to do with values. "About thirty to forty years ago when a Roman Catholic married a Protestant, it was a big deal. Now it isn't. Catholics, Protestants, African Americans, Whites—we all share more of the same values than we did back then, but we also have a higher divorce rate. There's something to be said for having the same values and the compatibility that goes with them. Could be that's what's wrong with our current system."

Inevitably religious holidays were brought in. Where does one spend Christmas, Hanukkah? A small-business owner remarked, "I don't think there is anything wrong with interfaith marriages, but marriage is hard enough. Some common ground eliminates one issue. Holidays end up being family and religious functions, unless you're an atheist. Short of that, the differences become an irritant sooner or later; yet people deny it's a problem. I have friends like that. What to do in the holidays becomes an issue, year after year."

These are men who want a woman to resemble them. That likeness takes different forms. A 45-year-old divorcé said, "I'm looking for a woman who best matches my own expectations, who has the same lifestyle. There are millions of women out there who have their own needs and values but don't understand mine. She has to understand mine. I mean, for example, I won't let myself go physically, nor should she."

Now hear what Stan Anderson, 26, single, Boyd Jenkins, 41, married a second time, and Leon Schwartz, 54, divorced, have to say about marrying for a common frame of reference.

STAN ANDERSON

Twenty-six-year-old Stan has all the qualities of an African-American prince: handsome, polished, charming, and accustomed to getting his own way. After graduating with a B.A. in music with a major in brass performance, Stan studied acting before taking his first real job in corporate America in Stamford, Connecticut.

At heart Stan is a jazz musician; he plays the tenor sax in smoky night-clubs or at church socials. That's his real life and once he nears success, I bet he'll give away those gray suits, suspenders and wing-tipped shoes he's so fond of wearing and don black leather.

Stan's parents have been married forty-three years. Stan is the youngest of three children, two sons and a daughter. He's single.

Stan's Sermon...

" The first thing I ask a woman I'm attracted to is how she feels about God. Maybe not straight out, but I'll manage to bring it up. I was talking to a drop dead gorgeous woman the other day and made a statement about the Lord. She came back with, 'All life is in His hands,' or some such cliché. I knew she said it for my benefit, not from her own experience. She just blew her integrity and everything else out the window. All she talked about was herself. I guess that's what she found valuable.

A woman has to have a relationship with God similar to mine, it won't work if she isn't Born Again. There are hundreds of Born Again women out there I wouldn't even look at; they don't have the belief I have. I can't base my life on the teachings of the Bible and then let some woman in who doesn't get it.

I look at Jesus' life as the ultimate in manhood. He has this image of power, of practicality, of integrity at any cost. A man of conviction. That's the kind of man I want to be: a man who can walk through life with no fear because he's walking in the truth. God doesn't call us to be perfect, but in God we are complete. It's a lifelong journey.

Ultimately marriage is also a journey and a process of becoming, it's not just who you marry. Let me tell you a story. A man who has had an impact on my life—he's a minister and writes books—got into a discussion with some other men about adultery. They asked him had he ever cheated on his wife. He answered, 'No.' They pushed him further, 'You've been married to the same woman for fifty years and never cheated on her?' He answered, 'I haven't been with the *same* woman—she's changed over the years, she's fifty years more beautiful, fifty years more intelligent...' He proceeded down this long list. It was a powerful testimony. It shows marriage as a plan that leaves room for change and inner development.

When I talk about change it's about me and the woman I marry moving toward the image of Christ. A marriage based on godly principles continues to grow and helps us move closer to each other. I want to be ten times the good man I was when I got married; I want my wife to be ten times the good woman.

That has a lot of implications. It means counseling other people with their marriages and doing all the things that go into Christianity, like helping the poor and really getting out there—not philosophizing or reading the Bible in the closet. Waking up in the morning and praying together, working in the ministry, going back to the neighborhood as the black couple who made it. If my wife had a totally different vision, if she couldn't agree to live this kind of life, it wouldn't work.

I'd like the woman I marry to have other things in common with me. You know, I put a lot of value in education and knowledge, and I don't mean to sound like a racist, but I need a wife who understands the frustration of a black man in America. It's more of a background thing. I don't want to be sitting down in the living room one afternoon and see on TV that another black kid was shot by a white cop and turn to my wife, 'Man, they're still doing that!' And she has a blank look on her face as if to say, 'What are you talking about?' I couldn't deal with that.

There's the image of what a black man is. When a client appears in the office looking for me, and sees that I'm black, he or she puts me in a box. I think I sound like a black man on the phone but some don't. They can't hide their surprise when they meet me. Like all black men are supposed to be on drugs or in jail! Those are the statistics. I am not being over-sensitive, I'm being realistic. Day in and day out, I have to tear down all the misconception garbage to build something new.

Diane understands all this. Oddly enough, her parents and mine were brought up only hours away from each other in Georgia and they, like so many blacks, left the South for better opportunities in the North. Our upbringing is very similar: we think the same, treat people the same, go to the same church. We're both the baby of the family.

What started out as a teenage romance at 17 developed into me finding a woman I could marry. We've been together for nine years. The whole time I have encouraged Diane to do her own thing. I believe in equality. You know there's no religious practice that puts women on a more respectable level than true Christianity. Last year she thought I was trying to get rid of her when I encouraged her to go to graduate school out of state. I wanted her to stay, but even more, I wanted her to get a good education. She needs to have her own money so she can have her own life. She gets out of graduate school next year.

I've already put my plan into action; I call it the three Cs— Co-op, Career, and Commitment. Christ is a given. First, I saved money to buy my co-op, and now I'm working on the career. I want to become a performer and continue to make moves toward that. Next comes commitment. Diane is important to me but marriage is a big responsibility. Now that she has concentrated on being the woman she can be and has prayed for me to become the man I want to become, I've changed. So has she; I used to say *if* we get married, now I say *when* we get married.

I have another story for you. Back to the minister. He was giving a sermon in church one Sunday and about twenty minutes into it said, 'I'm sorry, I have to stop. I can't continue without telling my wife she's the most beautiful woman in the whole world and that I love her very much.' He asked her to stand up in front of the entire congregation. The whole church erupted; people clapped and whooped with joy for what God had done for their marriage. He was really talking about the whole picture, and that story typifies how I want things to be.**"**

BOYD JENKINS

Forty-one-year-old Boyd looks like the solid citizen he is: squarish build, on the tall side, short brown hair parted on the right, interested blue eyes framed by Ben Franklin glasses. He attended a Quaker boarding school, graduated from college with a B.A. in art and sociology, and became a working artist.

A friend says he gives artists a good name—no affectation, no distracted musings, no inarticulate sense of time; he's organized, practical, realistic. Boyd creates graphic abstracts in his studio cum house on the outskirts of Santa Fe.

Boyd is the oldest of his mother's "brood" of four. He has two sisters and a brother, as well as two half brothers. His mother, now a widow, was his father's third wife. Boyd is married.

Boyd's Picture...

66 My first criterion is: Are we in the same racket? Do we speak the same language? Do we have common ground? That kind of thing. I narrowed it down to women who had a certain symbiosis with art, players in the field with active minds. I wasn't attracted to a woman who couldn't participate in the art world or integrate into mine.

In between marriages, I had a heavy affair with a woman I met while I was moonlighting at a hotel. Kay was really supportive of my efforts but had the least knowledge about art of anyone I knew. She wanted me to squire her around to galleries; explaining each show, letting her in on what the contemporary art scene was all about. She even volunteered to support me, but I was suspicious of her motives. She probably thought, 'If can help him out, maybe he might feel indebted.' In that sense I had to say no, partly because I'd have to spend too much time at exhibitions, plus I'd *always* know more. I mean, if I were a doctor, it would be ridiculous to teach someone who didn't go to medical school all the Latin names for the muscles, bones, or viscera. I wanted an equal with whom I could exchange ideas.

It's a funny thing, art—I'm attached to it to the core of my bones. It's such a demonstrative expression of my own identity that to be around somebody who's out of the loop would be like living with a stranger. Yet saying that, I can't live with another artist. I tried it once: there was too much competition, which led to plenty of friction and denials of commonality. You've got more going for you when your relationship is built on common values.

I thought I had that with my first wife. We were both in the art field so we spoke the same language, had a symmetry of looking at the world, even laughed at similar kinds of jokes. In its finer moments it was fantastic, wonderful. We were really simpatico. We'd lived together for five years and all the while Ellen was relentless about getting married. It was a lot of, 'Gee, don't we make a great couple?' I was left with those question marks, sorta like being prompted with conversational flash cards. So at 32, I finally said, 'Okay, let's go for it.' I figured the good times would just keep on rolling.

About the time we were making wedding plans, Ellen asked if her son could live with us. I really didn't know much about the kid since he'd been living with his father all those years. How bad could it be? But to tell you the truth, I didn't realize he was so screwed up and really violent. I got into fist fights with him; he once threw a bicycle at Ellen. This kid is bigger than I am! I did what I could, but eventually realized I had to leave. I couldn't take much more of the constant upheavals.

Getting a divorce took about two and a half years, in addition to the two years I spent trying to get out of my marriage. When the papers were signed and all the property went where it was supposed to go, I was legally free to do whatever I wanted. By that time I was facing 40. I wondered what to do. Maybe I should have kids? I should probably get into a routine. But if I lingered…it was like once you've fallen off a horse you have to climb back on again! I'm not trying to make light, but a certain percentage of such sayings are true.

I knew the more I stayed away from marriage, the less inclined I'd be to do it again. There is trepidation the second time around because you're all too familiar with the down side. You know what it takes to fight a losing battle in a marriage that's not working, you know how it feels to divvy up your assets, you're not naïve anymore. So when somebody comes along, no matter how perfect she is, no matter how rosy the outlook, you search for faults and find them. I guess it's just being self-protective.

And you test anyone who has the potential of getting close. My cat was a tremendous barometer of people but now he's gone to the litter box in the sky. Anyway, we hung out together and I really trusted his judgment. When I had friends over for dinner he joined right in, you know, pulled up a chair. I remember having a fling with a woman who was chasing me big time. My cat did his stuff in her pocketbook and on her clothes. In his most demonstrative way he cautioned, 'Go away, get out of here! This one has to go!' Finally I got the message and rid myself of that seedy relationship, but I wasn't always out to lunch. I mean, he endorsed most. He was instantly attracted to Lydia, my second wife.

I met her in 1981 through business; every couple of years, she would drop by to see my new work. We seemed to like each other but neither of us made any moves. We were purely professional. While I was getting the divorce I considered calling her, but then she offered me a show and through that context our relationship developed.

Once again, it came down to a parity of assumptions. Lydia and I come from a similar class, if I may put it that way, which made a *big* difference. I have an innate understanding of her values, so I don't have to guess at what's going to happen next— like I did with my ex-wife. Lydia doesn't say, 'Oh, you set the table *that* way.' There's no question because we both put the dessert spoon and fork above the plate. I hope that doesn't sound too stuffy.

In addition, we both know what our responsibilities are, who we are, what our roles are. And we both believe in fairness. Lydia works nine to five and has evening meetings, so it's impractical for her to do all the washing or shopping, and easy enough for me to plop the clothes into the dryer. You know, at times I *really* welcome the break. And when Lydia comes home, we can get down to doing what's really important: gossiping about the art world. It's great to speak the same language and understand each other so well.**"**

LEON SCHWARTZ

Fifty-four-year-old Leon is not very tall, has blue eyes, and is losing his fluffy white hair. After graduating from Drake University with an MBA in finance, Leon joined the Navy Reserve, and worked for his father before becoming a stockbroker in Boston.

Leon is outgoing, feisty, protective, and is an all-around good guy who gets upset at injustice: "I'll break up a goddamned fight in the street between twenty brutes and get killed in the process. I just can't look the other away when someone is in trouble." Yet on a personal level he withholds judgment, observing people intently before making any decision—pro or con—about them.

His parents were married fifty years; his father died recently, and he is the older of their two sons. Leon is divorced and has two daughters.

Leon's Outlook...

" I was very shy in high school. I never learned to dance and didn't smoke or do all those things that everybody else was doing, because of my home life. My father was very prudish: he thought if you kissed a girl she was a whore. I think he never liked women or was afraid of them. I'd watch all the guys jitter-bugging—we didn't have drugs and crap in those days—telling jokes, sitting with their arms around their girlfriends, sticking tongues in their mouths in front of everybody. They did everything I couldn't do, and had everything I never had.

When they started getting married, I was determined to find an unbelievably gorgeous woman. It was the classic 'I'll show 'em' scenario. The wallflower introvert who never had a date was going to come back with a woman who would knock them off their feet. And I did. It was the wrong reason to get married; better to marry someone less spectacular who has the same interests. But I was on a quest to find Madonna or whomever, and I found her.

Inga was a statuesque, blond, blue-eyed model going out with some society guy. I stole her away from him, quite an achievement for a poor kid from the training department of Waltson & Co. I wanted her and I got her, but not for the right reason. She was a possession. I walked down the street with her and everybody was jealous, 'Hey, look what he's got.'

I took her back to my high school reunion after the wedding. I was about 30. We sat with all those guys and their not-so-hot wives. They couldn't believe who I ended up with—the dufus and the beauty queen! We were married for thirteen years and had two girls. Lucky for them, they take after their mother.

The biggest problem we faced was not having common interests. Me being the outdoorsy type—although my belly doesn't reveal it—and Inga being more into opera and ballet.

There's nothing wrong with liking opera, it's very cultural, but I like rafting down a river or skiing better. After we got married I gave up my interests, which was great for a couple of years, but I missed doing my thing. When I resumed skiing Inga *only* wanted to go to the ballet, but being a nonskier, she encouraged me to go skiing on my own. I'm not a loner yet I don't want a ton of company around either, I simply wanted to share adventures with the woman I loved.

Sometimes infatuation takes over and you forget to get down to the nitty gritty of what it might be like to be married for ages. I know that happened to me. You need to know *beforehand* whether you share interests or enjoy what the other person enjoys. If you're really into tennis and your girlfriend isn't, find somebody who is. Otherwise you'll feel cheated. It's love –40 without her.

I'd like to marry someone who finds the great outdoors as fascinating as I do. Sure, everybody likes to go out to dinner or a movie but when I say, 'Hey, let's go camping or hiking…' Some prima donnas don't want to do that.

You need to have the same ideas about sex, too. A lot of people have the attitude that you get married today and what happened yesterday is no one's business. Maybe that's true, although what happened yesterday affects who you are today. You need to discuss what you like. I was engaged once at a young age, because I couldn't get into this girl's pants unless she had a ring on her finger. Her parents wouldn't allow it. That was the puritanical way we grew up. I'm sure if I'd been a parent in those days I wouldn't have let some slimy guy touch my daughter unless his intentions were honorable.

Those days were bad, but today things are different. People seem to be more mature; they discuss sex. A couple should agree about their sex lives too, whether it's doing it in the missionary position at 10 o'clock every Saturday night in bed or behind bushes in a public park during broad daylight. Otherwise the fighting starts and one or both begin looking around for some-one else. You also need a common understanding of each other's sexuality, and should think your lover is the greatest or one of the best, so that you can still get excited over the years.

I like the concept of marriage. There's something nice about it. I hope I've learned from the mistakes I made in my marriage. I know what went wrong the first time—we were too different—I think next time will be less problematical.

But I've been on my own for ten years and have had five long relationships that didn't end up in matrimony. I don't like one-nighters or going out with someone two or three times. Dating takes a lot of effort and I don't have time to spend juggling women around. I once went out with two women at the same time and all I did was worry about whose clothes were in my house and where could I hide the other one's toothbrush. But I digress. Those relationships were initially wonderful but started to wear a little thin once I took the rose-colored glasses off. I started seeing things wrong that I hadn't noticed at the begin-ning when everything was new and exciting—like she talked too much or wasn't genuinely kind. I played each relationship out; sometimes we just got tired of each other.

I've been very careful because I can't see getting married and then dividing up my assets again. The older you get, the tougher it is to have a woman come in and be part of your life, as much as you want her to. Suddenly things have to be done her way or you compromise. I know women who go crazy when I leave dirty dishes in the sink. They think I should wash them right away instead of letting them sit for a half hour. Big deal.

Maybe *I* don't want to change, who knows? You break up, go through a painful withdrawal and meet somebody else, hope-fully with whom you have something in common. Otherwise, what's the good of going white water rafting alone? I could tell people at the office about it, but they don't care.**"**

Seven

BEST FRIEND
"She's so comfortable."

"Besides, she's my best friend." I've heard that comment more than once and have never understood why one would want to marry a best friend. Don't we all have enough friends without having to marry one? Aren't we, by now, our own best friend? What is the difference between a best friend and a partner? Is it that the best friend likes you more? Understands you better? Let's you off the hook more quickly? Shrugs off disagreements because, after all, you're *best* friends. Of all the reasons men marry, this one was the most difficult for me to understand. I listened closely to their explanations.

Cody Smith started, "There are women you can sit down with and be totally yourself—with others you have to maintain some sort of facade." He told me self-consciousness disappears. Men feel more comfortable, more relaxed, more themselves with women friends. They don't have to be perfect, or near to it, all the time.

College is still an easy meeting place. A public affairs consultant who attended the same school as his wife said, "One night I really got stewed on some strange alcoholic concoction my roommates threw together, then we went for pizza. The combination proved disastrous. I threw up, not exactly in front of her, but she knew about it. Here we were on the verge of this boy/girl romance, and she saw me at my worst, my most foolish!" Fortunately for him, they had been friends first, so she knew he wasn't just another guy who drank too much.

There's a different awareness when men and women encounter each other attending night classes, serving on jury duty, or simply enjoying a coffee break together. They get acquainted without the underlying tension of, could this be Mr. or Ms. Right? There's no need to impress, nor is there a dating ordeal to contend with when people get to know each other casually. But the environment can change, as a 38-year-old explained, "Sometimes you admire a woman's sense of humor so much that you start hanging around her, then after a while you want to kiss her."

A bachelor said, "Usually the women I get involved with romantically start out as friends, *very good friends*. We form a mutual support mechanism. It's stable, enjoyable, and we have interests in common. I would much rather marry my best friend. How many people do you know who marry in haste only to find out they don't even *like* each other?"

And dating gets tedious. A 36-year-old complained, "Dating endlessly becomes an extension of work. I'm in sales and selling all day is like dating: trying to interest people, trying to smile, trying to keep out the negatives. You want everything to be happy and wonderful so they'll buy from you. You're *on* all the time."

Another bachelor admitted, "It's easier to get to know someone when neither of you creates an artificial situation. You've got to get away from that dating atmosphere. It's better if you meet on the job, or at church, or in a bookstore. You get to know each other as pals—without the time pressure of the first date, the second date, and so on."

I like the story a writer told me about a friend's long friendship, "For twenty years this guy was carrying a torch for a woman he'd known in high school, but she thought of him only as a friend—they even went on trips together, staying in adjacent rooms. In the meantime, she was involved with all sorts of clowns, but he stood by. A few months ago a light bulb must have gone off in her head because she realized she was in love with him. I believe he said something like, 'It's about goddam time!' They're getting married next week."

Although not all men marry their best friends, once married, they begin to regard their wives as confidantes. A fundraiser said, "Marriages go bad because the couple weren't friends. You and your mate should be best friends. Your relationship should be more important than her relationship with her mother, father, sister, or brother. You have to be number one."

Married for the second time, a 40-year-old rhapsodized, "Marriage gives you the opportunity not only to be a really close friend but to be a friend to someone of the opposite sex. It's wonderful to give and it's wonderful when it comes back to you. And you do this for each other. The companionship is really, I think, the pinnacle—and the intimacy. Everything from sex, to pillow talk, to having morning coffee, to taking little vacations when you go off by yourselves, to being in public together."

In the next pages we will listen to three bachelors, Peter Beckett, 28, Randy Williams, 27, and Keith Scoville, 29, all of whom plan to marry their bosom buddies.

PETER BECKETT

Twenty-eight-year-old Peter is of medium height, has soft brown eyes, and brown hair. After graduating from college Peter went straight to business school at UCLA, bypassing the work requirement because he had so much summer job experience. He worked as a strategic planner before moving to Utah for the mountains and the skiing. He's vice president of marketing for a big name resort.

Peter is gentle, easygoing, content and I suspect you'd have to push him pretty hard before he'd put his foot down. He drives a fifteen-year-old Spider convertible that he keeps running himself and since he can fix just about anything, he's in popular demand. Other pastimes include collecting native American artifacts and reading Anne Rice vampire books.

His parents are divorced; he's the middle son of three. Peter is single.

Peter's Transition...

" My mother and father aren't married to each other anymore. My mother is extremely independent, so I get the feeling that as long as I am happy, it doesn't matter to her whether I'm married or not. But my father has started to drop hints. He's the Jewish one! It's probably because my older brother just turned 30 and isn't married either. He wants one of us to get married and have kids.

I always thought I would get married. I think of myself as still being 23 and not old enough; lately I've started to accept the fact that I am getting older. I've been out of college for awhile and I'm more confident, responsible, more willing to have somebody share my life. Hopefully, I'll make the right choice the first time around.

I've run across a few people that I wouldn't have minded being married to if the relationship had been different. However, I haven't yet found that combination of love and friendship to be able to say, 'This is the one.'

It sounds crude and crass, but it would be sorta nice to have a 'ready-made date,' someone I could reach over to and say, 'Let's go to the movies tonight, honey.' I'd like a woman I would feel comfortable with, with whom I could share my thoughts and feelings. Having a woman in my apartment would be terrific and would certainly add to my ordinary routine. I have an idea from having roommates, but I know it would be different, not just taking up, but living in, the same space.

It is much easier to meet women in a sports or work setting. When you eventually ask her out you know that she is happy to be going out with you, not just to be going out. And she's not trying to appear perfect; you don't have to wait—like when you're dating—for the real person to show herself. Of course, those work relationships can get a little dicey. I dated my boss once—not the best idea in the world.

You know, we men like to have women as friends. I have a whole group of women friends myself. A lot of guys get to the point where they are faced with a problem; they look at a friend and wonder, 'Do I want to marry this woman or not?' You get comfortable and intimate in what you tell each other. The next step is an attempt to move the relationship forward and is very difficult. Like pole vaulting the Grand Canyon. It's not easy to say 'We have this great friendship, but now I think, uh, we need something else.' How do you join the emotional with the physical? I mean she could reject your advance *and the friendship*! It is the most delicate point because, let's face it, having sex changes everything.

That adage about guys only wanting sex may be true for some but I must admit once sexual tension is dispersed, you can get down to the business of the relationship. Sex just becomes another part of the relationship. Yet the further into the platonic thing you are, the more difficult it is to shift gears. It's almost as though you need to get the sex out of the way, *not for the sex* but so you can move past it.

There's that huge insecurity afterward for both, but if you're thinking about marrying your best friend, it's a damn worthwhile step and one you must take.**"**

Randy Williams

Twenty-seven-year-old Randy is medium height, with periwinkle blue eyes and cotton blond hair. He graduated from Louisiana State University with a B.A. in business administration, and joined an international property development company based in New Orleans, where he arranges financing for development and acquisition—factories in Budapest, apartment complexes in Milan, discount supermarkets in London.

Randy is extremely winsome and has a great deal of self-assurance, but underneath that smooth exterior is a man of iron discipline. For instance, he's at the gym by five o'clock in the morning and has a golf handicap of ten.

His parents have been married thirty-five years and have a two children; Randy and his older sister. Randy is single.

Randy's Awareness...

❝ I guess I fantasize a little about marriage. I mean, I hope it works and it lasts. It's finding a best friend. You get romance and sex, but day in and day out, you have a real good buddy. I have no grandiose ideas about what marriage will be like, because I know it's not easy.

I remember the night my father woke me up and said, 'Randy, I need your help. I'm moving out.' So he got the truck and moved the few things he had over to this little place he'd found. That was on a Sunday. My sister and I thought, 'Oh my God, what's going on here.' He travels a lot but when he came back into town on Thursday, he called me up and said he needed my help to move back in! He told me that I wouldn't understand what happened, but I guess it was something he and Mother had to do. So I don't have any delusions about marriage being a basketful of stars but I hope that's as bad as it gets.

I'm not going to fritter away the next twenty years of my life being hopelessly in love either. I'm planning to find a good friend with whom I can spend my life. You know fantasy isn't *always* some star spangled thing—it's a good relationship.

Take my sister's marriage. She settled down right out of college, relatively young. She and her husband were financially strained starting their own business, so when she got pregnant the bad times continued. I'm not talking welfare, but struggling. We both come from a privileged family, getting anything we wanted, so my sister had to adjust to a life she wasn't used to. I would watch her and her husband work things out, sitting on the curb talking and laughing, and sometimes arguing. Those two are a good testament. Times have been tough but their marriage never wavered because they like each other. They're good friends. They love each other and are *great* buddies. It would be so easy for either one to throw in the towel and find somebody else, but their commitment to each other keeps them going.

I'm looking for someone to marry sooner rather than later. My thoughts have changed recently. After I got out of school I wanted to make money. My job was very important to me; I was good at it and started to make a pretty decent amount. Now I can do most everything like travel or buy things. But all of a sudden I have no one special to share these successes with. I mean I did go straight for the money, working my ass off sixty hours a week—90 percent of my life is work. I'm starting to think that maybe I shouldn't be so focused on the cash, maybe I should take the 10 percent free time and turn it into 30 percent. Change the ratio some. Not stay in a five star hotel alone, but in a three star with someone I want to be with and with whom I can talk about my experiences.

I can't really tell you I enjoy dating. Often when I've finished work for the day, I'll gaze out the window into the lights, thinking to myself, 'What do I do now and with whom?' I have people I can run around with, but I'm at the stage where dating fifty women isn't very enticing. I've met women I've taken on weekend trips and so forth; they're okay. But if I don't feel a woman is for the long-term, I'd just as soon look elsewhere. I won't hang out with her simply because she's convenient. That all probably stems from the fact that I want to be married. I mean what's the point of starting up a long-term relationship with a woman I know I'm not going to end up with?

I met the kind of woman I want to marry. We lived together for two years. I loved her to death and still do. Caroline is just a great person. She was sharper and wiser to the ways of the world than women my age. She wasn't one of those 'come and show me what to do' types. She was ten years older, independent, and took no crap. She owned her own house and had a good business career. Caroline is strong-willed but sensitive, and isn't afraid to let her guard down. She liked being treated well by a man, and understood that just because a man is sweet doesn't mean he's weak. I was attracted to her because of her experience and low maintenance: she could take care of herself emotionally and didn't need constant reassurance. But her biological clock started to kick in. Frankly, I loved her and wanted children, but didn't quite know when; I had my career to think about and didn't want to find myself in the same situation as my sister. After a while we decided to part and go our separate ways. Caroline was a big part of my life but I lost her. She got married, had her child, and I had my career, so I guess things worked out well for both of us.

I'm nearly 28 and I've yet to find someone to marry. I've had some good times with women I like, but marry, no. I'd rather find that person or not get married at all, not for the sake of it. Some of my friends married because it was what they were supposed to do. They had to do it quick, almost to get it over with— get married, have the kids, make the money. Some marriages were based on lust and sex. Sex is great for the first couple of months, but they thought it was going to last in that context forever! You don't have to be a rocket scientist to figure that one out. I've had dinner with women when the conversation faltered because both our minds were on getting back home to the rack. But after a while it's only sex and how well can a relationship grow on sex? I don't think it can. I mean, hell, you can have sex with anybody.

I came the closest with Caroline to having that all-around relationship. We had so much together, plus she was a good friend. I recently had an affair with another older woman. She had a daughter a year younger than I. We had a great time but we were at different points in our lives. Would I marry her? No. I'm at the stage where *now* I want those kids and that house, but she's already been through that.

A few weeks ago, I ran in to a woman I was friends with in high school, and had gone out with a few times before we graduated, but hadn't seen in eleven years. I asked her to have dinner with me; it was as if someone had taken those years out of our lives and put us back together. I mean, it felt good. We clicked. I was pretty impressed: she has a career and her own home and is real gutsy. She wanted to have a baby but wasn't married so she decided to raise him herself. He's two years old. She was determined to do things her way. I like that and you know something? I've *really* taken to them both, so we'll see. **"**

KEITH SCOVILLE

Twenty-nine-year-old Keith has a slight build, blue eyes, and brownish hair. After graduating from Georgia State, he worked as a mechanical engineer in southern Florida before returning to Atlanta to get an MBA.

He is the boy next door: helpful, sweet, kindhearted. In fact, he lives with the boys next door in a group house reminiscent of college days. His roommates work while Keith commutes to his classes at the nearby college. He plays the role of social director for his friends and just started planning a "White Trash" party, complete with tuna casseroles, Wonderbread, and a Spam carving contest.

Keith's parents are married and have three sons; he is their youngest and single.

Keith's Pals...

" I've never been very good at picking women up in bars; it's the worst place to meet people. Everyone is on their guard, trying hard to project some image. It's all so pretentious. I've never been the type who picks up a woman, then goes on to have a really 'meaningful' relationship. It's never worked that way for me; I'm better off acting like myself instead of trying to put up a front. That's why I usually meet women through school or friends.

I have plenty of friends; I'm really into group activities. When my friends said some of the girls I dated weren't for me, I had to consider their perspective. They said these women weren't well suited to me—too reserved and not spontaneous— compared to me, Mr. Outgoing. After a dozen or so semiserious relationships, I have finally noticed a pattern and guess I'll have to make a midcourse correction. Maybe I'll have to look for someone who can be my best friend, who's a sport, who also has a lot of friends and is extroverted. I've gone out enough to notice similarities between women: I'd meet one and she reminds me of another! Well, not exactly in the same category, but close to the same spectrum. Time for a change!

Look at me, I'm still living in a house full of guys leading very much the bachelor life. I have played around. I lived on the beach in Florida and really had a fantastic time—parties, surfing, rollerblading. I see myself getting married at about 32. I picked that age because I will have done enough by then. At 24 I wasn't too concerned about marriage, but now that my 30th birthday is ten months away, it's time to move on to the next phase of my life. So getting married is moving up on the priority list.

I think the positives of marriage outweigh eternal bachelor-hood by light years. But while you're single, you're a fool if you don't take advantage of the freedom—the ability to just take off and do what you want. How could you not exploit those options? Otherwise you'd miss out, that's why some guys see marriage as the proverbial ball and chain.

I'd marry a woman because she was my best friend, someone I couldn't live without, someone who is passionate to be the best doctor in town or the best den mother. We might buy an older house and fix it up. Both of us could work on it, learn together about wainscoting and dry rot. I see myself as a man for the '90s; I have an open opinion about the roles each of us would undertake. None of this man out working, woman at home baking cakes. No moving to the suburbs, driving a station wagon. That's all too constraining—but I would like a dog.

I have two women in my life: Dawn and Janice. Dawn and I had this off again–on again affair; I was fairly serious about her. She used to go out with some guy who reappeared on the scene and asked her to marry him! She gave me right of first refusal, but I passed. Ever since that day I wonder if I really screwed up. She married him and a year later, he was killed in a water ski-ing accident off the coast of Mexico. It was a tragic story. I have been in contact with her to see how she is doing, but I am afraid she's not doing well at all. I feel so sorry for Dawn, it was quite a shock, but the truth is—the first thought that popped into my mind was—is this fate? She's not ready now, but I wonder if I'll get another chance.

Then there is Janice, who has been a pal for ten years. We dated for awhile four years ago, but it didn't work out because the transition to dating was too difficult. We continued to keep in touch, you know, told each other about the people we were dating, and now that her live-in just moved out, we're seeing each other again. Things are really heating up, but I'm not too sure where that relationship is going either.

So in the meantime, I'll continue going to school, writing my papers, studying for my exams. Who knows, maybe I'll meet someone in one of my classes—I still have a year to go until graduation.**"**

Eight

LONELINESS
"The silence drives me mad."

In l989 a survey conducted by R. H. Bruskin and Associates concluded that men are twice as likely as women to cite loneliness as a motivation for marriage. Yet one hears more about the unattached female going home to her cat, spending weeknights with David Letterman, and Saturdays out with "the girls," than about the lonesome guy who bores his married friends with tired jokes and lingers past midnight. Men admit to hating solitude, we know they get tired of dating, and Randy Williams told us about those times when he asks himself, "What do I do now, and with whom?"

What is the alternative? Hanging out with the guys, frequent trips to the video store, endless dating? After a while it all gets fairly predictable and stale; the idea of slipping into a solid relationship starts to play on the mind. As a 41-year-old said, "Now that I am getting up in years, the whole idea of growing old with somebody becomes a comforting thought, a wife to fill my needs, the spaces and the holes: the loneliness—as long as it doesn't lead to bickering with each other all the time."

Granted, loneliness can strike at any age. Some men marry right out of school or after a tour in the service, because without a support system they're lost. However, many of these marriages are consummated before they know themselves or their wives. Rarely do they last; couples grow up and break up—each flying solo.

Being alone is unsettling; the silence is frightening and keeping in touch with the world outside by watching television or listening to the radio is voyeur-like. Men find "things to do," staying an extra hour at the office or buying season tickets to the Celtics, getting so engrossed there's little time or room to feel that sense of detachment creeping in. It's a good defense, but strangely, more solitary than staying at home, dreaming about a special relationship.

However, not all men jump into an early marriage or hide behind escapist behavior; some are bound and determined not to spend another weekend painting bookshelves. An entrepreneur told me, "I'd like to marry so I can stop worrying about the isolation, what to do with the rest of my life. I'm so preoccupied with living alone. It's a real distraction and I don't know how to fix it. I'd like to use my mind in other ways. I read magazine articles about being single in the '90s—it's not like the '80s, when everyone was going out more. All bets are off." He continued, "There are even more compelling reasons to be married; I'm lonely and I don't want to die lonely; I'm scared and thinking about mortality; the world is so cruel and I am all alone in it. That would be marrying by default, but it's not any less a reason."

Age can be a factor, especially for men in their late 30s and 40s who watch people pairing and re-pairing. A copywriter said, "I'm 45 and right at the crossroads. I never thought about retirement or old age but those issues are becoming more and more important. I understand more why people decide to marry: so they can grow old together and take care of each other."

A 41-year-old mused, "If I stay single, I am doomed to an image of a lonely old guy who is always invited to Thanksgiving dinner. I'm the hunched over uncle without any children who is grumpy but nice. All my fourteen nephews and nieces love me, but wonder why they don't have an aunt."

Like a jack-in-the-box, those empty feelings pop out when least expected. A chance meeting with a widower from across the street or breakfast with a co-worker who has been out on one blind date too many serves as a marker for the future. One observer commented, "The fear is that as you get older there are fewer and fewer people available. I mean, do you want to spend your old age alone? Look at the widows and widowers who don't have any choice, even though they were happily married for a zillion years. Now they have to face the prospect of living alone for the rest of their lives."

A single man in his 40s said his dying father lamented over and over, "What do men do who aren't married? They don't have anyone to love them or come to the hospital to take care of them. What happens to them?"

Lonely people achingly notice how full life is for married couples. The dread of always standing on the outside and peeking into lives they wish for themselves can be overwhelming. A man who's been divorced for twenty years, although he's had countless opportunities to remarry, told me he declined a good friend's invitation to spend Christmas Eve together, because seeing him with his family would be too much of a reminder of his own emptiness. Instead, he spent the evening in seclusion with his books, listening to the Beach Boys on his CD player.

A bachelor observed, "Single people are always complaining, 'I can't believe how much time this is taking.' Married people are just the opposite: they are very aware of how short life is. I mean, they can't believe how fast the kids have grown. They say to their friends, 'I can't believe my son is shaving already!' Their memories span their son's entire lifetime."

Marrying as an end to interminable loneliness is the eighth reason men gave for finding their way to City Hall. John Combalier, 42, and single, Benjamin Hannon, 41, and divorced, and Gordon Laurence, 55, and a widower, share their feelings about being on their own.

JOHN COMBALIER

Forty-two-year-old John is about six feet, with dark curly hair and hazel eyes. He's put on weight and it shows in his black, Day-Glo inscribed "24-HOUR CHURCH OF ELVIS" T-shirt. John dropped out of the University of Pennsylvania after three years, lived in Spain, and now lives in Seattle where he works as a freelance proofreader, editing new editions of classic works, young adult novels, and science fiction.

John is completely at home with the unconventional, almost preferring it. He's active in the underground cultural fringe and is friendly with many people writing for alternative publications. As hobbies, he collects old paperback detective stories for their covers and plays classical guitar.

John's parents are divorced. He has a younger sister and is single.

John's Experience...

❝ Friends tell me I should get married and I say, 'Well, fine. Send her over!' Quite simply, I'm not married because any woman I wanted, didn't want me; any woman who wanted me, I didn't want. That's a facile answer, probably rather obvious. Until now I haven't concerned myself much with marriage, but I'm beginning to think, 'Well *I am getting older*, I mean, am I just going to go on dating *the rest of my life*?'

Dating is a trickier business when you're getting up in years. There's a different slant on that younger, older, or women same age choice. For instance, younger women are more adventuresome but not much into dealing with older men; older single women are more demanding and forthright. They tell you, 'I've been through this relationship and that relationship. If you're the man for me, let's talk, otherwise forget it!' Not a great deal of accommodation there. Women in their middle or late 30s, or early 40s are in the same category as older women: they've experienced enough to define their parameters. So that narrows the field at both ends, leaving me in the same boat as older women—I take what I can get!

Which means either I find a fresh young thing who likes a man 'with experience' or I fit into a snappy older woman's predetermined ideas. Whereas if I were younger, there wouldn't be as much resistance to overcome. Of course, I could bowl a woman over: 'Wow. I never thought I could fall for a guy like him. He's not at all like what I thought I wanted.' Sure, dream on.

Awhile ago I had an affair with a married woman. It made me confront head-on two aspects of marriage; I was on the outside observing her marriage, wondering what it would like inside, married to her. What looked like a steady, tight marriage consisted of two people alienated from each other—that's why Tamsin started the affair with me. She just about gave me an engraved invitation to 'come on down'; although I hesitated, eventually I gave in.

Her husband was very French about the whole thing: 'I don't want to know about it. Treat her nice. Don't embarrass me in public.' Fair enough, but you can't tell me it's not traumatic when your wife is sleeping with another man. It was difficult enough for me. We got to the point when she had to decide whether to break up with her husband or not. It was 'or not.'

I was an emotional disaster and more or less had a nervous breakdown; couldn't eat, couldn't sleep. I'd sit all day long staring into space, barely uttering three words and when I managed to, my voice sounded wistful and sad. Then I wanted to smash things, completely flipping out. Slowly and painfully I recovered, but it took a couple of years. I guess that adage is right— the time it takes to get over a relationship is equal to the time in the relationship.

Now I'm fine but I get lonely. I have a lot of female friends but I'd rather have a relationship beyond mere friendship. I just can't bum around with them forever. How about a little romance or sexual attraction? I know those are not synonymous, but they are tied up with each other. How about a woman with intelligence, unconventional, with a quirky sense of humor? I'd like one, please. But if she likes Billy Joel and doesn't get Elvis, forget it!

Beyond that, I don't know. I'm a workoholic. The deadline factor takes over my whole life, like having ten term papers due in two weeks. So most of the time I don't have the energy to cook. How bad could it be to hear, 'Dear, I've prepared a delicious dinner for you tonight.' I have a conflict about that, it's sort of MCP* thinking, plus the women I know aren't into playing housewife.

I think I've found the woman I described. However, there's the question of how to get this thing going—from acquain-

---

*MCP—male chauvinistic pig.

tanceship to friendship to romance to serious involvement. It's not merely finding her, it's the actual going out and doing things together that's so dicey. If I did connect with her, I'd have to give up my solitude. I know that for some guys that might be a big negative, but to me it's really positive. I probably spend too much time alone anyway."

BENJAMIN HANNON

Forty-five-year-old Ben is medium height, with blue eyes and gray hair. After graduating with a bachelor of science in forestry, Ben ran his own home-building company until the market turned sour. He currently works as an independent insurance agent from an office in the local shopping mall.

Ben is one of the few eligible men in a small Tennessee town, and everyone seems to know him either through business, his little theater group performances, or from church. He sings in the choir, and among the sea of blue robes, it's not difficult to spot this dapper man shyly watched by the women in the congregation.

His long-married parents have two sons; the elder, Ben, is divorced and has two teenage children from his first marriage.

Ben's Lesson...

" I've always been married. I depend on having a lady around—to eat, drink, and sleep with. Marriage gives me a sense of security, of comfort; I admit to my fear of being alone. The only time I was single, except now, was in college. But then I lived in a dormitory with lots of people around. It's really frightening being on my own. Somehow I've got to learn how to function without a woman.

I married twice for all the wrong reasons, or at least in my current state of mind it looks that way. I married my first wife at 23 because I couldn't face the big bad world. How could I graduate from college without a wife? After all, we'd been dating for three years and it seemed the thing to do. I married Betty because Rona, the lady I really loved, was already taken. I loved Betty, too, of course; we were married for twelve years.

I was 35 the next time I married, not long after the divorce. Let me say I *always* wanted to marry Rona, except that once. I've known her all my life: we grew up together and in our freshman year she decided we should get engaged; but as it was too soon for me, she married someone else. We dated each other in between her marriages. I kept going back to her like a bear to honey.

Rona has been married three times, I was her fourth. Finally I got my turn! When Rona came to town and moved in with me, she was regarded as 'the other woman.' We lived together for a few months, but since such behavior is frowned upon in our small community, we tied the knot. We wanted to be socially acceptable. Rona is such a charmer that she won over most of her detractors, and we were invited to join some of the right clubs. That's quite a compliment, you know.

During our nine-year marriage, Rona worked in a gift shop and at what I call other menial jobs. She had a college degree but didn't think she could better herself. I helped her look around; I was the one who read the want ads and talked to friends. I thought if she didn't have to work all those strange hours we'd have more time together. Finally she found a good job and left me! Said she didn't need me anymore. Rona has a new boyfriend younger than her who doesn't make as much money (he does commercials or something). She must want someone to control.

My second divorce devastated me. I ask myself, if something like this could happen again, who can I trust? It's the first time someone walked out on me; I walked out on Betty, never understanding how bad she felt. Now I do, and believe me, paybacks are hell.

I'm in a period of transition, just dating around these last seven months. I've been out with five different women. I'm looking for a lady who has a good sense of morals and is honest, caring, loving, and communicative. My priorities have changed in the last year, so these qualities are far more important than just physical attractiveness and chemistry. I'd like to know how she was raised, what her values are, what religion means. Previously, I looked for dependent women. My father was a dominant person so I was probably following in his footsteps, but I am not sure I need to be needed anymore. Look where it got me with Rona.

I guess if I found the right lady I'd marry again, maybe living together first. I don't want anyone having keys to my house right now. I can ask a woman to stay, or I can ask her to leave; I can go to her house and if I'm tired of her company, I can go home. At least I've become that independent.

The woman I go out with more than the others has some of the attributes I'm looking for, but not all. She meets the communication, sincerity, and love parts, and because those are high on my list, I'm overlooking the rest. I like her but I don't think our relationship is going to lead to marriage. She's aware of this too, and you know, I'm not sure she's so interested in getting married either. We have been going out for two months only but have agreed to keep an open mind to see how we get along. As far as I'm concerned it's a good arrangement. I'm still smarting over Rona and I need to handle being on my own, at least for awhile.**"**

GORDON LAURENCE

Fifty-three-year-old Gordon is tall, with hazel eyes and dark hair. He was born in a suburb of New York City but has lived in Miami most of his life. He has degrees in mechanical and industrial engineering and is a partner in an environmental consulting company. Gordon's colleagues regard this pleasant man with affection, although he's not the easiest person to get close to. It's his interests that amuse people: he's a big fan of the Lone Ranger and relishes old-time radio programs. He once flew to Lone Pine, California, the site of the television series, to celebrate the Lone Ranger's sixtieth anniversary and recently attended a local radio convention, carting along posters, comic books, hard cover books, radio tapes, and magazines he'd collected to trade and sell.

His mother is a widow. Gordon has an younger sister and he's a widower with a son and daughter both in their 20s.

Gordon's Precision...

❝ Shortly before Jennifer died, she told my son and daughter, 'I want you to make sure your father is not alone, make sure he goes out and dates. You've got to push him out of the house. I don't want him vegetating; I want him to marry again.'

Jennifer was sick four years and during that time, I used to think if I ever lost her, I'd be better off staying single. I thought I was *very* self-sufficient and well organized. *I* wouldn't have any problem living alone emotionally. After her funeral, my children made good on their promise and didn't leave me alone for six weeks. They rearranged their schedules so that one was home with me every night, but the time finally came when I faced being alone. The inevitable Saturday night rolled around, and to tell you the truth I wasn't sure how I was going to handle it—so much for my great ideas of self-sufficiency! But I did, by climbing into bed at 10:15 and going to sleep.

I could be by myself every other night, but three or four nights in a row was impossible. After about six months I realized that I'd never be good at being single for another thirty years, yet alone another three. I need to share life's joys and pleasures, even troubles. You can't talk to your kids all the time and I didn't want to hold them back. They have their own lives to lead.

My children were pleased when I started dating again. In fact, they joked about my dating habits. I was out maybe two, three nights a week with a different woman, and they admonished, 'You can't 'casual date' just because you did that thirty years ago. You're supposed to pick one woman, then when you finish with her, date another.' Twenty-year-olds giving me advice!

I remember right after Jennifer died, friends we had known as a couple would call to see how I was doing, but that was about it. A few invited me to dinner, but only *my* very closest friends asked me to go out with them, to take in a show or movie. When I started dating, how people changed! Suddenly I heard, 'Oh, why don't we get together?' A whole realm of socializing opened up, just like when I was married.

I was introduced to every one of the twenty-two women I went out with either through singles ads in the local papers or blind dates—everyone offered to fix me up, even my father-in-law's girlfriend! One day I was thumbing through a copy of Jennifer's *The Jewish Week* and found a singles page, so I answered those ads too.

I met some fairly substantial types, mostly professionals. You know, when I was married, I used to fantasize about different women in the office. I know now those fantasies kept me going during Jennifer's illness. I thought, if she dies and I'm left alone, I'll at least have these women to call. I wasn't looking forward to the idea but it gave me comfort. However, when push came to shove, I didn't ask them out. I was already going out on blind dates and answering ads. I found an army of women who had nothing to do with work, who were closer to the kind of woman I could get along with, and who were head and shoulders above the women I had only a year earlier thought were *so* attractive.

I went out with all sorts of women—one was a prison guard and a nudist. She told me she was 46. After I told her how old I was, she admitted to being 52 but said she shaved a few years off for the ad. She said men don't like to go out with a woman who has the big 'five' in front of her age. Not me, I have no need to walk around with a 35-year-old on my arm to show I'm a man. I have much more in common with a woman approximately my age, a woman with some of the same experiences, who can look back and laugh and talk about politics or movies. What would I do with a 35-year-old, a nostalgia buff like me?

I knew by the third date whether or not I wanted to pursue a relationship. I was looking for a good sense of humor because after all, I do some pretty crazy things. An easygoing personality was second; third was intelligence. I didn't want to talk down to anyone. Fourth was a sense of adventure. I have no specific physical requirements, so I went out with all sizes and shapes; if I had any preference, it was for tall, since I'm six feet two inches.

I think I might be in love again. It's too early to tell yet, but I'm beginning to lose interest in dating. I answered Barbara's ad in *The Jewish Week*. All she said was 'Very attractive widow likes fun and adventure, seeks successful male 52 to 60.' I wrote her a letter, enclosing my picture. She called me Sunday night (that's when most called) and said, 'Hi, it's Barbara.' I had just written to a friend of Jennifer's named Barbara, so I asked her how she got my letter so fast. The mail must be improving. She said, 'What do you mean? We live in the same city.' Whoops, that was a little awkward.

Anyway, we got to talking and an hour and a half later we made a date. I immediately liked Barbara when she said, 'Let's have a drink and if we don't get along you don't have to buy me dinner or anything. We can go our separate ways.' After dinner, I was surprised when we kissed goodnight—most of the other women just shook my hand. That was the beginning.

I'll be ready to remarry along two lines; number one, I want to wait two years out of a sense of propriety, although traditionally one year is enough. Number two, I need to know if sufficient time has gone by to make sure I'm no longer interested in dating other women. If I could pick up a newspaper and not immediately turn to the singles page, if I could say ' No, thanks' to a friend who says, 'How would you like to go out with this hot dish?' Then I would know I was getting close.

Maybe there's a third: my children would have to get along with whomever I choose. They're a major part of my life and I would like them to approve of her. They're both astute and sensitive, and if they didn't like her, I'm sure there would be a substantive reason why.

My kids have met Barbara a few times and like her. I haven't met her two children but they are older, 30 and 29. She had her children by her first husband when she was 22 and now is a grandmother. She didn't have any by her second. Just think, if we got married, I would be her third husband. And you know, there are days when I really do think about putting my house up for sale and moving in with her.**"**

Nine

SOCIAL ACCEPTABILITY

"My world is made up of couples."

It sounds almost Victorian to hear that men still believe they need a wife to be socially accepted. By whom? And who really cares? Men do. They don't like being left out of the social and business swing because of their marital status. Single and divorced men remember occasions when they were not invited to "couples only" activities. Such rebuffs are not intentionally dismissive but are simply a matter of numbers: two by two. Remember when widower Gordon Laurence was excluded from the social fray and was included *only* when he was able to produce a woman?

A recurring theme of man as the fifth wheel appeared throughout my interviews. The popularly held belief that an unattached man is *always* in demand and is *more* welcome than an unattached female ain't necessarily so. One man about town summed up what many told me, "We live in a couples-oriented environment and as you get on in years, it's even more so. I overheard a conversation between friends who had gone to a movie I was hot to see. Three couples went together and there's a damn good possibility I wasn't invited because I wasn't hooked up with anyone. By and large, people aren't as apt to invite a single person to an intimate party, and in business, the couples thing hits you again, because whether you're working with the wife or the husband, both usually appear at social functions. At big number industry cocktail parties, it's fine, but when you give a dinner for seven people, there's a different balance and people notice it."

When counted along with the other reasons men marry, the need to pledge one's troth for acceptance by some *outside world* seems fairly shallow, at least on the face of it. You'd think that having a significant other or living together would be enough to satisfy those Noah's Ark bean counters—but it isn't. A 29-year-old bachelor said, "People are very uncomfortable with the unmarried; they never quite know what to do with you. My brother lived with his girlfriend until they got married, and I remember the huge rows between him and my parents about who was going to sleep where. And when I worked for a bank, their policy allowed single people with *ten* years' employment to invite a 'guest,' but if you were hired the same day and married, your spouse was automatically invited."

A divorcé at 40 confided, "I don't like living together. I've done it. It's a limbo state. Socially, it's not great. You set up a household and do everything as a couple, but have no legal status. In Western society a man needs a wife for social reasons."

And to join the club. When you think about it, marriage is like an exclusive fraternity or sorority. It has the pledge period (the engagement), initiation (the ceremony), insignia (the wedding band), and special acknowledgments ("My wife"). Sometimes even blood is let!

Once married, perspectives change. A newly married 36-year-old is surprised to discover, "I spend more time with married friends than with single friends now—and I thought that would *never* happen. Single people who want to remain single are comfortable around me, but those desperate to get married feel uncomfortable because they're so frustrated."

The corollary to marrying for society's sake is that a bride has to adapt to her groom's lifestyle. She must "fit in" with his circle of friends and business associates, be it eating donuts at the local social club, waltzing at the charity ball or playing softball with the sales force. An unmarried 28-year-old identified such characteristics: "I know this one girl who is really corporate wife material. It's a horrible thing to typecast someone like that, but she puts together a great dinner party, makes intelligent conversation, is a member of all the 'right' women's clubs, and all that kind of stuff." And an entrepreneur admitted, "It's really not my style to ask anyone what they think, but when I first met Carol we drove back in the same car with some of my more difficult friends. It's relevant having someone who understands the social nuances, because from time to time, we're all with other people and it helps if your companion makes the effort."

Marrying for social acceptability is not just lightweight talk for Will McDonnell, 45, Steven Elkin, 38, and Don Scardin, 32.

WILL McDONNELL

Forty-five-year-old Will is five feet nine inches tall, has dark amber eyes, and is just about bald. After being laid off from his job selling computers in a large department store in Virginia, Will, at the ripe old age of 44, returned to college to complete a degree he started in his teens— before Vietnam got in the way.

Will is attractive, easygoing, affable, and loves to talk. His great passion is inventing, and if any design or mechanical problem is mentioned, Will is likely to come up with a solution. His other passions include flying, building hot air balloons, and designing programs for his Macintosh computer.

Will's mother is dead; his father remarried. He is the younger of their two children, a daughter and son. He is married and has a six-year-old daughter.

Will's Odyssey...

❝ The year I decided to become socially acceptable again, it occurred to me that marriage could bring back a life I had left years ago. If I could unite with another person, I could unite with the larger world. I had to find a way to return. I'd been on the outskirts of society for so long I couldn't even see the landmarks anymore, let alone follow them; I needed a guide to lead me. I lived in Alaska, among other places, and believe me, that wilderness metaphor works.

I married Sharon to integrate into society. Friendships weren't instructional enough and I had so much to relearn. It's like having a mountain of things to do and doing one section at a time. I thought if I married I could proceed from there.

All society is contractual: if you want to work for me, then we have to agree to do it a certain way. Marriage too is a contract. If you can't buy into marriage, with its few written rules, what do you do with the rest of society? Marriage is the easiest because there's just one person to satisfy—you treat her with respect and learn to get along. So that was my first step. Next, I had to figure out how we both fit into the community as a couple.

I dated lots of women, figured out what they needed, but couldn't satisfy them sexually, or they had more ambition than I did. When I met Sharon I realized I could accommodate her needs and she was willing to take me at face value, but I'm getting ahead of myself.

It took me years to get over a traumatic college romance. Of course, I became involved over and over again with others, but felt guilty because my heart belonged to Beth. I was haunted by that failed experience. Friends told me Beth had married and divorced, so I tracked her down. I talked her into letting me come over to her apartment. When I saw her I was taken back; I didn't know her at all, didn't recognize any of my feelings for her. I thought we might resume where we'd left off eight years ago, when I left college to avoid the draft. I was looking for a past I couldn't find. After we spent that afternoon together, I realized I had to let go of that dream, to literally change directions.

I got on my motorcycle and rode to Michigan, where friends had asked me to join them. I planned to put my past, even the good memories, behind me. I was going to start over, begin reconstruction, rejoin society. I found a place to stay in Michigan, got a job as a cook, and was really doing well. I thought, 'Hey, I can start over.' No one knew or asked about my dropping out.

But my new life came to a halt when my mother was diagnosed with cancer and died nine months later. I couldn't believe how quickly she departed this world; it was so unfair. Life's finiteness really hit home and somewhat unnerved me.

On the other hand, discovering how fragile life is, and knowing I could start over, encouraged me to continue my new life and look around for a wife. Not all of this happened overnight, mind you, it took me a while to come to these conclusions. I even found someone but she was too recently divorced to try again. She had spirit and was really independent, but thought she'd have to give that up if we got married. I don't know why she thought that way, I like a woman with a mind of her own. Unfortunately, I really couldn't pursue her as much as I wanted because I couldn't find a better paying job.

So I moved back to Virginia to be near Dad and was hired by the local department store on the highway. That's where I met Sharon and was attracted by her willpower, something I didn't have. I think relationships are like owning a business—you both need different skills. I mean, I wouldn't hire all accountants. I admired her strength, and her ability not to be overwhelmed by other people's demands. In many ways I'm easily intimidated; she is not. Clearly marrying someone with these qualities would be a useful union. I could learn from her and cultivate these qualities in myself. Sharon is also realistic; I lack that perspective. She has her own personal structure, a road map leading to a larger universe; if she could follow it, so could I.

I'm not so sure what Sharon thought of me but I had to keep her interested. She would have backed away in a second if I hadn't kept believing we were going to get married. When I said, 'I would like...what do you think about getting married?' she was shocked, she hadn't expected my question. I think I appealed to her responsible side.

Over the seven years we have been married, my life has improved considerably; I've put down roots, I'm part of a community, I have a wonderful daughter, I coach elementary school soccer, I live in a nice house. It wasn't so great getting laid off after eight years but with Sharon's emotional support I returned to college last year and am now making all *A*s. The future looks bright. **"**

STEVEN ELKIN

Thirty-eight-year-old dark haired Steve was born in Paris when the Salk vaccine was unavailable and consequently has been in a wheelchair since child-hood. After getting a bachelor of science in accounting at Fairleigh Dickinson University in New Jersey, Steve and friends started a nationally known electronic business, making him a millionaire by his early 30s. He now acts as marketing director for a discount outlet, just for the hell of it.

During the day, Steve usually can be found wheeling around the sales floor answering confused customers' queries or gently ordering his staff around; at night, he's out on the town, dining in French restaurants or hanging around the latest "in" clubs. He appreciates nothing more than a good bottle of Bordeaux or a good-looking woman.

Steve's parents have been married forty years. He is the older of their three children, two sons and a daughter. He's single.

Steve's Dazzlement...

❝ I've been ready to get married for six years. I've been on the lookout but it just hasn't happened. Every time my pals meet me I'm with a different woman. It's tough on them and on me. I want the stability of having a wife so I can be part of my old circle again, most of whom have moved on in their lives. Those friends are very important to me, as we've grown up together and shared so much. We used to get together regularly, but now they have kids and travel around in couples. I'm left with my new single friends, most of whom, by the way, are younger— because if you're single and older that's who remains.

Everybody tells me about all the women 'out there.' I hear it all the time, all this talk about biological clocks, women wanting to start families. Well, I'd like to have children and certainly have enough money. It all sounds great, a regular computer model, but in reality it doesn't work. It didn't with the last woman I was seeing and I don't know why. I'm not so sure women know what they really want. I need to meet the one who has some idea; maybe I am not meeting the right girls?

The ones attracted to me don't want to get married. A woman with marriage on her mind looks at me and wonders, 'Could I marry *him*? Can he have sex? How long is he going to live? What would we live on?' She has a different vision because I'm disabled and she doesn't understand what she can't see.

So when I meet somebody and get a response, I tend to get involved. I accept a lot of what's on the surface and don't dig too deep. If she accepts my situation, then I accept hers. That's one of my faults.

I go out with good-looking women, tall, blond, striking. I've *never* gone out with a Plain Jane or even started a conversation with one. In my teens I was fortunate to meet very interesting women. It felt good to me, almost like I could walk, when people said, 'Wow, how did you meet *her*?' I don't know, maybe that's what's wrong. I've been out with sevens, tens, and elevens. Although I'm more comfortable with a seven, I've never felt that a woman who is not beautiful had other qualities to make up for it. I'm very prejudiced about beauty, but I can't help it. Whenever I'm with a pretty woman, all of a sudden everyone wants to know me; all of a sudden I'm treated as an equal.

I have gone out with hotshot models and dated an actress once. They were all inadequate in some part of their lives and looked at me as some sort of link. In a way, I think they were envious. I mean, they thought if I can make it, not being able to walk, then maybe they, with all their perfection, could find contentment. Sometimes I'm not so sure these are the ones I should be dating. They seem so fey, not real.

I figured out what I'm looking for in a wife but I just wonder if such a woman exists. I don't care if she wants to work or wants to be a housewife and stay home playing cards, that's her choice. I'd like her to be mentally and emotionally supportive and I'll be supportive back, and I'd like her to be adventurous and bright. My last girl wanted to become a writer and I gave her money to study. But she went off with some guy she met in class! So trust is important too.

I am the guy nobody fixes up, the guy in the wheelchair. I have two strikes against me before a woman ever talks to me, but I'm a nice guy. Once you get to know me, the wheelchair disappears—but few women cross that boundary. Other men have problems but theirs just aren't as visual. With me it really is, what you see is what you get.

Living in northern New Jersey isn't so easy. I've lived in other parts of the United States where people are friendlier, more open, less superficial. I might have to quit, completely change careers, move to a different environment, maybe get into the counseling field, or open a little coffee shop. Of course

I'd be the owner, so I wouldn't have to be tied down to it. Basically I can do anything I want to do. I work to keep active.

I'd rather be married than anything, but I'm reaching a point where I can't analyze what's wrong anymore. I'm confused; relationships aren't like making business decisions. They are much more complicated. I want the convenience of being married, of being part of a couple, having a family. I have gotten fairly close but then something pops up that I hadn't anticipated and it's over.

In retrospect, I still haven't met a woman who wants to travel in the same direction as I do. I won't marry someone I've just met since I'm not one of those guys who says, 'Let's get married tomorrow.' I'm not that stupid or that desperate. But I am surrounded by happily married couples and it would be nice to be part of that scene."

DON SCARDIN

Thirty-two-year-old Don is tall, with black hair and brown eyes. He grew up in Alabama and graduated from Alabama State with a degree in economics. After a stint in the Army, he sold houses, but currently works for a building management company.

Don has a real down home friendliness that masks his ambition. His competitive style shows more on the baseball field than in social situations, where he tries to be smooth and silky. Don lives in one of those huge apartment complexes in Birmingham, complete with security guards, a golf course, swimming pools, and parking spaces filled with sports cars.

His parents are married and have six children, three sons and three daughters. Don is the oldest and single. His brothers and sisters are all married.

Don's Expectation...

" Society pushes you to do what's right, and the pressure's on me to get married. I'm not getting any younger; I'd better find myself by the time I'm 36, otherwise something's wrong. By the time I get married and have a child I'll be an old codger! There's truth in society's ways, the right and wrong of it. If I don't get married pretty soon, life will pass me by and then what will I have to say for myself—I blew it?

I can't think positively about a man who, at 46, is still on his own. He could be the most brilliant professor, a man who gives his knowledge to the world, but I'd wonder what he's done with his life. Society points the way. I know it changes, but basics are basics.

I can't give you an estimate of the number of women I've had. Two hundred scares me, but one hundred seems small. It sounds like a lot but it's been seventeen years and I've lived with four different ladies. The first two were brief, when I was in the Army, young and wild, having a great time. Between 22 and 25 I went out with too many women. I knew I couldn't do that forever: it gets old after a while. I wondered if living with one woman would calm me down, how it would feel to wake up to the same face every morning. I lived with the third one for a year and three months.

At 26 I was dating again. I dated my present girlfriend four years before we moved in together. Miss Junior League. I guess I was waiting for clap of thunder to signal 'This is it.' But I don't think either one of us has heard it—after all, we've been together six years. I'm moving to another apartment soon and will *never* live with another girl. Next time I'm getting married.

I don't recommend cohabiting—it's just buying time. I have a friend who was going to set up house with his girlfriend but I cautioned him against it. I knew he wasn't making a commitment to her or society. People move in together for the wrong reasons, like convenience or finances. We live by certain traditions, one of which is marriage. So when I conform to everyone's expectations and get married, I have a hunch all sorts of things will be attained—a mature relationship, a family, acceptance.

I'll be looking for a stylish lady with good looks and a good body. It would be best if she loves me like my mother. If I could get the feeling a mother has for a son in a spouse, it would be awesome, a constant high. But quite honestly my mom has gotten fat. I can't imagine how overweight married people look at each other. They must have incredible self-confidence about themselves and each other. You know, I'm strong and fit at six feet 170 pounds and I look forward to waking up every morning next to a woman who's as physically healthy as I am, who I'm happy to be with, bad breath and all.

But the better the body, the lower the emotional quality: what you get in one place you lose in another. The prettiest ladies have a tendency to get the best things life has to offer and tend to be snobby, less caring and less trustworthy. The finer the lady, the bigger the headache. I know guys who have gorgeous bombshell girlfriends, but they're as evil as can be. I can't imagine them cooking anything eatable; better to stick with a more wholesome type woman who is pleased to be with her man.

After I leave and get settled, I'll be back on the circuit again, going to cocktail parties and the ballet, out on the town where I can meet a lady like I want, when we're all dressed up and lookin' good. Society's alarm clock is warning me to get in line and my desire to find a bride is getting stronger, so I'd better get a move on.**"**

Ten

FREEDOM
"I can be who I truly am."

Let's talk stereotypes once more. Men don't want to give up their freedom—those late nights with the boys, or the "girls," for that matter; doing what they want, when they want; pigging out on Doritos; throwing dirty socks and newspapers on the floor. Freedom is seductive but not all men are fooled by soft candlelight. A single 38-year-old observed, "It's interesting, freedom. We finally get it and find we now have the opportunity to walk out of an open window or into a manhole, without anyone trying to stop us. We're free enough to do something really stupid and detrimental, counterproductive and self-destructive."

Along with illusions of free play come derogatory comments about The Dragon, Godzilla, The Management, The Little Woman, She Who Cannot Be Denied who interferes with a man's good time. An astute 25-year-old recalled a boss who referred to his wife as the "the ball and chain" in front of business associates, but the young man knew for a fact that the boss called his wife at least three times a day, and she rarely called him. Outward bravura, inward need?

A twice-married man admitted, "When I was divorced, I was much less organized, less directed, less purposeful. Sloppy. I forgot to send birthday cards to my family. It was pretty chaotic but now that I've remarried, life is smoother. I even work better."

Stereotypes have a modicum of truth: men *and women* give up a certain amount of self-determination when they marry. Or do they? Could marriage actually bestow freedom? We're not talking contradictions here because marriage does offer different choices: a way to plan the future, an opportunity to develop a particular talent or interest, a framework for personal development. Marriage can release men from their isolation, from constantly being on the hunt, from too much self-involvement.

A man who marries for freedom looks for a woman who will give him autonomy or is flexible enough to negotiate the boundary posts of marriage. She might encourage him to expand his horizons, or at least won't stand in his way. She may want her own space, not being particularly interested in lassoing, tying up, and branding her partner.

However, Russ Farrell, 39, Gene Nyland, 43, Barry Jacobs, 53, all of whom are married, and single Donald Yates, 37, can explain marriage as not being penned in better than I can.

RUSS FARRELL

Thirty-nine-year-old Russ is big and sturdy, with graying brownish hair and green eyes. He's from Minnesota, but since graduating from the University of Chicago with a masters degree in public policy moved around the United States and Europe. Now that Maine is home, he works as a welfare reform and income distribution analyst.

Russ is tolerant, genuine, and big-hearted—always willing to listen and help with other's problems, but not to the detriment of his own goals and ideals. His sincerity and cordiality bring out the trust in people. He is likeable and straightforward.

His parents are married; he is the middle son of five and is married.

Russ' Challenge...

❝ I have a very different view of marriage—I see it as liberation. The Greeks had a word for it, *Enantiodromia*. It means running into opposites: the act of commitment brings liberation. It's an ironic but relatively well known phenomenon.

Traditionally men are taught to see marriage as this *heavy duty* commitment. They wail about all the things they have to give up, like staying out late and so forth, but a different kind of liberation comes from meeting your responsibility to your wife and to your marriage. It's a struggle, but by attempting to honor the commitment, somehow in a funny way, it allows you to transcend yourself.

It is not easy to explain, but if you're fortunate enough to have a wife like Louise, you can get in touch with what's good about yourself and by the same token, examine your short-comings. We all have to face our own contradictions, our nastiness, our selfishness. Marriage allows you to view these things through another person. It's like holding up one of those magnifying mirrors found in swanky hotel bathrooms. At times I don't want to take that close a look! No one should do it *all* the time.

But you know, those evenings when I feel like saying, 'To hell with her, I'm going out for a beer,' or if there's a prolonged silence in the apartment, instead of acknowledging that the reason for this tension *may be* my fault, I get kind of surly. Eventually I face up to the fact that the problem may have nothing to do with Louise and everything to do with me.

I try not to act like that very often because I like to be around my wife, and by the way, I'm also disentangled from all that crap associated with trying to meet someone. That might sound superficial but it is nonetheless important to me.

I guess some of my liberation was also brought about by an untraditional marriage to an untraditional wife. Louise is a Lt. Colonel in the Air Force, so when we exchanged vows I knew we'd have a different lifestyle. But the most interesting part is that I chose *this* woman, I didn't choose a traditional woman. My marriage is very unlike what I hear about; it's less structured—we both accept our roles, but then we'll drop them and take on the other's. It's taken me awhile to become comfortable with these exchanges.

Like my brothers, I was bred on the romantic view; you met a nice girl you liked, got married and the whole experience was wonderful. You know, flowers, candy, kisses, the whole thing. Very predictable, a way of life our parents had, with clearly defined roles, the woman in the background, doing housework, writing out thank-you notes. If she worked outside the home, her position wouldn't take precedence over the man's job. I guess that reflects common notions about marriage—which is a load of crap. I always got the impression that the wife was really pulling the strings, all the while mouthing things like, 'My husband's the boss.'

I'm certain most men wouldn't put themselves in the position I'm in—where the wife's career takes precedence, or to put it another way, man sacrifices job for a greater good. I remember when we drove over to tell Louise's family about our engagement. Out of respect and because I wondered what it would be like, I went though the whole routine and asked her father, 'May I have your daughter's hand in marriage?' I remember him saying the usual, 'I hope you can support my daughter in the manner to which she has become accustomed.'

It was nice to say, very old-fashioned and totally irrelevant to our relationship, as we were both making the same money. I knew Louise was going to be transferred again, which meant I'd lose my job with a consequent loss of income. To me, our relationship had more to do with how we are with each other.

I have a lot of admiration for Louise—she grew up in a more conventional home than mine—yet is less encumbered by what's so called 'acceptable.' You know, I love to cook and Louise doesn't particularly enjoy standing in front of a hot stove after work, so I do most of the cooking. It was one screwy role in our marriage, and for the longest time I had this internal fight with myself, 'This isn't right, she should cook.' It's only in the last eighteen months—and here's another example of liberation—that I've felt at home enough with myself to be what I am, a damn fine cook.

I remember my wedding day, standing outside the church having a cigarette with one of my brothers. He asked me if I was nervous and I lied, 'I'm only nervous because of all these people here.' But I had good reason to be nervous. Life is difficult; it's harsh. It's not easy to come to terms with yourself, but the opportunity to encounter yourself always exists, and having a good marriage gives you the privilege to pursue it, if you have the guts.

The longer I've been married (that's eleven years) the more I realize I had no concept of what marriage was like. After all these years I've finally put it together and it's *really* good; it's about a growing acceptance of who I am and who Louise is, and that's never finished. **"**

GENE NYLAND

Forty-three-year-old Gene is tall and thin, has brown hair and light brown eyes. He grew up in a small "burg" in Missouri, and before getting a degree in literature served in the Navy and the Peace Corps. He's a fire fighter in Oklahoma City.

Gene usually looks tired because of those late night alarms—fire fighter to the rescue! His face, full of concern, is just the one you'd like to see peering over the top rung of a ladder. Reassuring and strong, he's also been called to break up domestic fights and has witnessed more violence, strife, and heartache than most.

His mother is a widow; Gene is the sixth of her twelve children, nine sons and three daughters. He is married and has a nine-year-old son.

Gene's Route...

" I was a romantic at heart. I wanted to roam the world, to experience everything on my own. I kicked about. There was no room for a wife because I never wanted to be responsible or faithful, so at least I was intellectually honest with myself.

I joined the Navy right out of high school and traveled around Asia, then signed on with the Peace Corps for Africa. I wandered all over northern and some of eastern Europe before going back to school. While I was fancy-free and living about, I had lonely periods too. When I saw an extraordinary mountain range or a dazzling waterfall I thought about how nice it would be to have a woman with me to share these wonders.

But it didn't help much that I'm shy, not one for socializing. So I didn't meet many women on my own. I'd most likely be introduced through other people or run into women at large gatherings like weddings or parties. You know, one thing leads to another. I'd catch her eye. Then maybe go a little further and talk some. If her voice was pleasant then I'd have more interaction, ride it for as long as it goes, become social, ask for a date. I wouldn't think about getting serious until we were well into it.

I was never moved to marriage but I had an ideal. I figured I wanted a woman, not a dependent. So if I died or left, her heart wouldn't skip a beat because she didn't rely on me. Also, I didn't want to impress anyone; in fact, I wanted a woman who was comfortable with herself, who would fit me into her already busy life. We could be mutually independent; that is, if I could find somebody who'd go along with my vision.

I lived with women, but most of the time for convenience. If there was any kind of relationship it wasn't very deep. It was casual. I didn't enjoy living together because it isn't approved of socially or morally, and you don't have any rights. It's too insecure, like not being fully vested. No one brings anything to that kind of living arrangement other than, 'Maybe I'll be here tonight, maybe I won't.' And I didn't care for that, so I kept just about everything loose.

When I was in college I lived with a nurse for a few years. It started out great, then dwindled. She had all these goals and what not; I was a student and had no idea what I wanted, let alone could imagine what the two of us would become. I destroyed the relationship by allowing it to disintegrate, by becoming not exactly mean but less attentive, taking the cowardly way out. I did another woman a favor by letting her move in with me because the local housing wasn't so good. She had a very busy job and was hardly there; she stayed with me almost to have a mailing address. We had casual sex but there was no love or anything that would have led to matrimony.

I came to Oklahoma City to visit two of my brothers. I needed to support myself, so I found a job and just started living here. I worked as a bartender, in the post office, just to be working. I wasn't sure what I wanted to do but then I got into the Fire Department and I liked it quite a bit. I met Fran through an acquaintance of my brother's while I was looking for something to do.

She appeared to be just what I needed: a few years older, independent, not a ball buster, and modest about her own achievements. Fran was on a career path set up by her company and I got the feeling she could live without me. She was not at all impressed by her own earning power. I mean, it wasn't a fortune, but it's more than I had. I was doing well just to take care of myself. Shoot, she wasn't interested in my money, I knew that straight off 'cause I didn't have any!

We were at dinner one evening, when I talked about how I was damn content with the way everything was going: my job, us, living in Oklahoma City. I naïvely said, 'How could it get any better?' Then she told me! Fran agreed that she was generally content and happy, too, but we *could* be married. It knocked me back. You know how you say things off the top of your head and sometimes you're sorry? I mean, I hadn't even considered marriage.

Afterward I decided Fran was probably right. I mean, she put her cards on the table: 'Well, if we did, when could we?' Six months later I was a married man. And not too long after that, we had our son. And here I am, ten years later, still okay about the whole thing.**"**

BARRY JACOBS

Fifty-three-year-old Barry is six feet two inches tall, with dark curly hair and brown eyes usually hidden by aviator glasses. He grew up in California, got a bachelors in art and his MBA, and settled in Philadelphia after working in London. He owns a small financial advertising agency.

Barry brims with schemes, and is creative and relentless. Funny and infuriating at the same time, he enjoys being controversial: it gives him a larger than life profile that helps business but at the same time, puts off close friendships.

Barry's parents are married and he is the younger of their two sons. He's married and has a two-year-old daughter.

Barry's Find...

❝ I married Erica because she was the first woman who accepted me for who I am. I didn't marry until I was 44 but had four live-ins. Women always wanted to change me, each had in mind what *her* man should be: more loving, more successful, monogamous. I could have lied and pretended to be someone I'm not, but I've never been very good at those coy male/female relationships. I am who I am, and what I am is not particularly likable because I believe that *other* women are important. I see someone new and my tongue hangs out. That's my nature.

I used to think, 'What man in his right mind would get married when there are so women to play with?' Some men play golf or sail in their spare time, but my sport was jumping into the sack. Marriage was no great reward. On the other hand, I had to change my mind because I could talk about sex with Erica just like I could with another man. I could tell her how I felt when a woman peddled by on a bicycle and her skirt blew up over her waist. Verbalization is half the exercise: talking about sexual desires helps me from acting on them.

Other women I went with packaged love, sex, and marriage together. I didn't include love with marriage, nor did I equate sex with marriage, nor sex with love. Sex is sex. Love is love. Marriage is marriage. Women always judged me. If I was interested in somebody else, I wasn't interested in them. I never asked a woman to be faithful, how could I? That's not reality. They wanted me to be jealous but why should I? Either you have a relationship or you don't. When a woman talks all night with another man at a party, it's irrelevant because if a relationship is working, it's strong enough to withstand flirting or fooling around. The advantage I got when I married Erica is that I could have her, and be myself, no matter how disgusting!

The problem is people marry anticipating their sexual relationship will be the same as it was at the early stages; whereas everything gets more complicated with children, with houses, with jobs. Look, it happens in every relationship I've ever seen. Men mess around on their wives and don't tell them. They pretend to be devoted husbands yet they fornicate with strangers. If one partner needs sex, then it's the job of the other to support him or her. If my wife wanted lots of sex, I would make sure she got it, even if it meant going out to get it. And vice versa. There is no sense denying that these things don't exist. If you need sex, you need sex. If you need rest, you need rest. If you need to read, read. If you have an honest relationship you work it out; otherwise, frustration sets in.

You have to be who you are. Marriages break down because of dishonesty and because people enter into them with expectations not likely to be fulfilled. For instance, when I married Erica, starting a family was the last thing I wanted to do; I had no wish to reproduce myself or carry on the family name. In fact, we had agreed not to have children but then she changed her mind. We battled and battled. Of course, I gave in. Where would I find anyone else so accepting? Now we have an adorable little girl.

At 17, I was confined to a hospital bed for months with a crippling injury. I was a suntanned, happy-go-lucky kid, who no longer took physical good health for granted. It forced me to change the way I looked at myself, dramatically. I had to adapt to different ways of getting around and I guess that started me questioning everything. I studied psychology for years, working on personal development. I couldn't stand being a weak, suffering man maintaining a facade, afraid my whole life. The key to living with myself was coming to terms with who I really am, so now I truly am who I purport to be. That doesn't mean I'm incapable of playing games when I need to, just that I prefer not to.

After I graduated from college, I traveled to Europe and realized I wanted to live there and get involved with northern
European, not American, women. I wanted to have a woman
who was a strong human being, yet feminine. American women
are nobody's fools but they've lost their femininity. I don't mean
they are not attractive because they are. I appreciate that they
are clean, bright, and intelligent, but they don't see themselves
as women; they're not sure who they are. When you meet a
German woman, she may be as hard as nails but she exudes
femininity. French women see themselves as female first—the
way they walk and hold themselves—but they're also tough
cookies. European women never hold you for ransom sexually
the way American women do, always expecting something in
return. I know that's a broad (no pun intended) generalization,
but it's a good one based on years of experience.

I met Erica first when she came for a job interview. Then I
met her again in one of those self-help courses. We were both
in the advanced class, so got to know each other really well. I
saw her in between other women I was dating, and I lived with
her for about a year and a half before she suggested making our
arrangement permanent. I, of course, thought it very unwise,
but while away on a trip, got to thinking: where else would I
find someone this unique?

She was what I wanted, Scottish, maybe a little young—
23—but nice, friendly, attractive, generally wonderful. And
most importantly I knew I wouldn't have to go around the rest
of life pretending, because she wanted me, warts and all, and I
could talk to her about *everything*. So we got married nine
years ago.**"**

DONALD YATES

Thirty-eight-year-old Don is of medium height, with dark brown hair and blue eyes, and has recently grown a beard. He lives in Florida, where he attended Florida State, getting a B.A. in English. He worked for newspaper and book publishers before starting a small design, layout, and print business ten years ago.

Don's conscientiousness, determination, and flexibility make him a good business person. He works long, hectic hours, losing track of time in an effort to produce perfect brochures or ads. On his few days off, he daydreams, mulls over ideas and design solutions, and writes for a music magazine.

His parents have been married forty years; Don is the eldest of their three children, two sons and a daughter. He's single.

Donald's Hope...

❝ Everybody has dreams in adolescence. Some men think they kiss them good-bye when they march down the aisle. I mean, what if those dreams were really important ? What if you were a really good writer in school and wanted to give winning the Pulitzer prize a shot? Why should marriage be a distraction?

I look at marriage as a springboard for accomplishing so many things. Why couldn't your wife say, 'Hey, honey, you really want to write? Why not give it a try, you've got the freedom, the support, and the love to make it happen.' It goes for both parties, it includes the children, everyone who's part of the marriage.

The sum is greater than the parts: two people get more done as a unit than as individuals. And I don't mean that materially, like making home improvements or something; it means bettering your life. Having another person around is *not* detrimental to personal growth and expansion. In fact, being married can unlock doors that were locked while single. If it's a good marriage and both husband and wife go about it creatively, all sorts of matters can be revealed, matters each didn't have a clue about.

Like maybe one person always wanted to play the piano. 'Oh, are you going to play the piano? Do you play?' 'No but I have been meaning to.' 'Oh, I love piano but you need to practice a lot.' 'But it's so boring.' 'But no, no, wait. I know a few chords myself.' And then two people start working on it, you know? Two people can actually keep an interest going. 'Hey, I've heard you practicing and you're doing better.'

And it's said out of genuine concern. If your wife knows you have an interest, she can provide a gentle nudge to keep you going. 'I don't want you to get into a funk. This thing is important to you and I'll keep you interested because your happiness is important to me.'

I'd like to get married. It has to be *the* big challenge—actually having another person in your life. But it's also such a risk, it's easier to shy away. Bachelorhood is so easy. When people describe getting married as taking 'the plunge,' it must be true. Getting anything good requires uncertainty and a willingness to take a chance. I guess that's how I felt when I started my own business. I worked for other people for so long, and made them look good for so long, and watched them get rich for so long. When the opportunity came, instead of staying safe on board the corporate ocean liner, I lowered my rowboat into the water.

I mean, unless you are neurotic or great harm was done to you, getting married is certainly worth trying—and failing—than not trying at all. I wonder what it would be like to be a husband? Would I like to be a dad? I know people who think marriage is restrictive, but they're not being creative enough. I look forward to having the freedom to come up with the kind of relationship best suited for me or us. Once I have that, I could just get on with my life.

I'm working on that in my current romance. I used to live with another woman, Roberta. It felt like marriage; when we broke up it felt like divorce. But now that I'm with Amy, I can see my former relationship had so many constraints to it, just the opposite of what I'm trying to build.

Roberta never cut me any slack. Say if I was running late, I wouldn't call because I knew she'd say something like, 'Well, how come you're late? I've been waiting all day!' And I was late anyway. So when I'd show up she'd rake me over the coals. I'd stand there like a dope, looking at my shoes mumbling, 'You're right, you're right, I should have called.' But most of the time I was just postponing further recriminations.

And it left scars. I fear negative reactions so much that I don't communicate. Roberta used to think fighting was the sign of a healthy relationship. You know, getting your feelings out in the open. Fighting is *not* a sign of strength; it indicates failure.

If we had a strong relationship, we wouldn't be fighting at all. Fights happen when things don't work. What could possibly be healthy about that? When you watch two people arguing with each other on the street, do you think they are admirable, that they're communicating?

Even now, I tense up when I find myself in a situation that would have previously, provoked a terrible fight. I get ready for it. And you know, Amy *doesn't* fight with me. I just want to hug and kiss her and tell her how wonderful she is, not to have whatever it is be a problem.

I'm getting the feeling Amy may understand that a man can be a diamond in the rough. We aren't all cut and polished like Prince Rupert in *Hearth Fires of Passion*—or whatever those romance novels are called. If a woman thinks she has found Mr. Right, she should dust him off and marry him. He will grow as a result of being married. He may even be looking for a reason to change, if treated fairly and loved. After all, people go to college and come out differently.

I think it's strange that all those romantic movies *end* with marriage. I mean it's really a beginning. Marriage is dynamic. If two people are attentive and creative, then they will change, hopefully in a way fulfilling for both. After a few years, they might even look back and say to themselves, 'Was I really like *that* when I was single?' **"**

Eleven

TURNING POINTS
"Whoops, I changed my mind."

For some men "Get me to the church on time" has a different meaning. It's more like "Get me to the church *some time*." They're simply late bloomers; it takes longer to figure out who they are and what they want. Or they wait until their careers have taken off or certain professional goals are met. Identifiable passages can be charted: coming to terms with parents, chucking out a roommate, letting go of rescue fantasies or romantic idylls.

For others events may be more dramatic: a parent dies, they're fired, change jobs, or wind up in divorce court. And some find it difficult to settle down with one woman, marrying frequently and making inappropriate choices. After a broken marriage or two they begin to take stock and examine the mess they've made of their lives.

Undoubtedly, such behavior devastates the women who love those Romeos who run away, afraid of emotional closeness or the commitment needed to build a life together. They start to see other women, become inattentive, explaining, "It's just not working anymore. It's not you, it's me." And they're right!

Various men were able to pinpoint an event or time when their attention turned to thoughts of marriage. After passing through what I call turning points, they understood themselves better, found more appropriate mates, and interestingly enough, these "ultimate" marriages are successful because they're more firmly grounded in each man's reality. We know about serial marriages, but in talking to men in depth, it became clear that many first marriages were practice runs. A deep commitment wasn't made. Remember Mark Galeano's comment: "I married the first time because it was what you did. Quite frankly, I didn't know any better."

How do men reach their critical turning points? Some seek psychological counseling because they can't face another broken relationship. Others finally realize they are not doomed to repeat their parents' or friends' destructive patterns. Still others meet a woman who is so perfect that a wedding becomes irresistible, or they "connect," to quote Mark again, "with my feminine side so I became more comfortable sharing the emotional parts of myself with women instead of just the physical."

Less evolved men can be propelled by fear, trading the fear of a future alone for fear of commitment. This is particularly true of men over 60, some of whom are convinced they face the choice between marriage or a nursing home.

On the following pages, Greg Lechinko, 43, married for the third time, Alex Snow, 48, married twice, and Martin Ranieri, 49, married once, recall what changes lead them to wear a boutonniere, and Jonathan Potter, 28, single, describes the goals he must reach before walking down the aisle with his bride.

GREG LECHINKO

Forty-three-year-old Greg is one of those tall, blue-eyed men who looks younger than he is, perhaps because of his dimples. He grew up in Vermont, got a law degree at George Washington University and now works in nearby Baltimore.

He has an old-world courtliness and charm that make it difficult to believe he's a lawyer. He's a frequent concert goer and plays Vaughan Williams on a Yamaha grand piano, reads biographies, humor, and books on baseball. Greg makes macabre jokes; for instance, when the city put up bridge railings in an attempt to deter suicides, Greg looked at them and said, "We need to put up a sign: Good Bridge One Mile North."

His mother is a widow; Greg is the youngest of her three sons and is married.

Greg's Shock...

" I changed because my father died. I was 39 when I realized it was about time I grew up and prepared for the future. I had very few people to turn to for solace; several close relationships had unraveled. All those people leaving made me acutely aware of my unhealthy emotional life. I wasn't being as loving or as caring toward my friends. I was leading a playboy life, deceiving myself—and the women I got involved with—that I wanted to marry them when clearly I did not.

My father's death was just the jolt I needed, I hate to say. I was *so* alone. That time of sadness and agonizing self-reflection over a three- to six-month period seemed never to end, but led to a fundamental change in my value system, in the way I viewed women and marriage.

I've been married *three* times. The first time I was young, 20 years old. I was very much in love with a woman I met my last year in high school and we married our senior year in college. I don't think either of us realized we were going to turn out to be very different people. I wanted a wife with me when I stepped out into 'the real world,' a very dangerous place for a man of going-to-war age. I wasn't sure whether I'd end up in Da Nang or law school. Talk about insecure! I didn't know very much about life then, and to this day I'm amazed by people barely out of their teens who marry and survive long enough to be happy. Getting married wasn't a bad choice; it was an experience I had to have, a mistake I almost had to make. It didn't damage either of us permanently. We just didn't share the same vision anymore about how to live our lives, either separately or together, so we broke up after three years.

After the divorce, I dated and had an extremely emotional affair with a woman who would be unavailable for days, disappearing to Atlanta or some such place with her girlfriend. She was seeing me and another man at the same time, but didn't inform either of us. Couldn't make up her mind, I suppose. I was depressed, knowing something was wrong but not being able to put my finger on it. Finally I talked to a woman psychologist who pointed out that, 'She must have someone else and isn't telling you.' I was very surprised. When confronted, she admitted the truth but didn't think anything was wrong and that *really* hurt.

Clearly, I had a lot to learn about women. I was shockingly naïve. I thought all women were good and those few bad ones were easy to identify, like Bonnie in *Bonnie and Clyde*. It never occurred to me that women would find it convenient to lie. I thought men had all the character defects, while women were in the mold of grade-school teachers—all perfect, never making mistakes. It took a few hard knocks to realize that women come in the same varieties as men—positive, negative, shades of gray.

At 27 I married on the rebound because I found a woman who was serene, stable, and steadfast. You might say I went from one extreme to another. I equated inner contentment with a placid demeanor, but didn't bother to check underneath the surface. I'm pretty emotional myself, and need to talk things out, but my second wife never confided what was bothering her, nor did she deal with any of our problems, or even allow herself to get into a healthy argument. Instead, she'd hide. Our house conveniently had an upstairs and a downstairs independent of each other, so she'd lock herself away upstairs. I guess she'd sneak down late at night to the kitchen to get food, then get up early to leave for work. Maybe I wasn't in love with her enough, because after awhile that marriage wasn't important to me anymore; it didn't last two years.

After my second divorce, I *really* felt like a failure. I had a sense of diminishment as a person, as a man. I'd had two marriages that died and I blamed myself. Every time I was in a new relationship, if it wasn't absolutely *perfect* I wouldn't take it any further. And it bothered me that I had been married twice. Women would ask, usually on the second date (you know what the conventional moralities are about dating—you sleep with the person on the third date because you've discovered in two dates they're normal, or at least not psychotic) 'Have you been married before?' And I'd answer, 'Yes, when I was 20.' Of course it was a half truth. By the time I felt the person knew me pretty well and there was something of value in the relationship, I'd say, 'I want to tell you a little more about myself. I've been married twice.' The reaction I usually got was, 'I wish you had told me before.' And I'd say, 'Yeah, but you brought it up when you barely knew me. If I'd said I'd been married twice, it might have scared you off.' The unanimous response: 'Yes, you're right!' It became a tried-and-true formula.

In retrospect, I didn't want to remarry, but I sure thought I did. If you'd asked me I would have said, 'Sure, but I just haven't found the right woman.' There was another fantasy I had to get over—the perfect woman. She had to be good (of course) and had to come equipped with tremendous talents, like being entertaining, brilliant, and athletic, not to mention beautiful. However, in my lifetime I've found the one thing you cannot expect—in a spouse or anyone—is perfection. I guess the best way to evaluate yourself is to measure how far from perfect you are.

So all through my 30s I had a few relationships and dated. Friends were under the illusion it was easy for me to meet women, but I was extremely shy and had a hard time. I tried personal ads—both answering and placing them. I tried going with appropriate male support to bars where single women were known to hang out. I tried gallery openings, any place where women might be in droves, where I could reasonably talk to them or say erudite things in front of crappy paintings. I don't think any way to meet women is out of bounds. You do whatever works. The worst that can happen is that you're embarrassed or you have a long, never-to-be-repeated dinner.

For me, the beginning of any relationship is verbal. Then you start experiencing things together, like going out to dinner. Eating is the next best thing to sex—superior to it, some claim! An erroneous viewpoint but... You know what kind of restaurant to take a first date to? A ribs place. That is, if she's not a vegetarian. You can't have good manners eating ribs, so you don't worry. The worst place is some fancy restaurant where you order Cornish game hen and spend the entire evening picking little pieces of flesh off the bone, trying to look really suave.

Then comes the sex part. I used to say to myself, 'I am going to sleep with this woman because I *could* marry her.' Maybe it's my upbringing or my own way of rationalizing what was going on. Ah, those Elizabeth Taylor relationships, the potential for marriage was always there. I really deceived myself, because in the long run, my glandular reactions overruled the logical part of my brain. Also, when I was physically attracted, I had to remind myself not to miss the obvious; I once went out with a woman who was gay and it took me months to figure it out that, well, she was bisexual.

From the time I was 39—months after my father died—I set out to find a wife. I realized that I needed someone intelligent who had both an artistic and a conventional side, like me. People who observe me ambling down the street probably think, 'Ah, Republican, suburbanite!' Friends who know me well say, 'Left wing, deviant!' Whenever I took out a woman who was too conventional, my pals would warn, 'Don't even think about marrying her. The only challenge you'll have is deciding where to go for brunch.' I eventually found a woman who had that unconventional side, but was less evolved. She had taught in Peru. She was certainly more liberal than her parents, and came from an old line family—lots of money, you know, the large house with a study filled with first editions.

Her family was superficially happy when we announced our engagement, but after handing the ring back, she confessed they weren't *that* pleased. They worried when I dressed in black, afraid my clothes reflected something weird about my personality. All it showed was that I look thinner in black! So maybe that's my neurosis. I like to think I have a James Dean side. I thought she had one, too. I probably could have rescued her from a life of conventionality but I was too pissed off. However, that fiasco turned out to be the best thing that could have happened, because I later met someone much better suited.

I was 42 when I met Joan through work. For two years different people told me I should meet her. I said 'Sure!' but then they'd tell me the timing was off; she was getting out of her marriage or she was dating someone. Then we were assigned a case together. It took us about an hour to start passing notes in the middle of an otherwise boring deposition. We had lunch the first afternoon, dinner the second day. It took off very fast. We had similar backgrounds. She was smart and had been married twice before. Joan also has an advanced degree in economics and a pretty good position, eventually she might be more financially successful than I am. She's eleven years younger. What's the Herman Tarnower equation? The ideal age for a woman is half yours plus ten. Doesn't elicit much sympathy for the late doctor does it? Luckily, I have the energy to keep up with her.

We married a few months ago and probably acted too quickly, but we'd lived together for a short time and felt so comfortable with each other it seemed such a natural thing to do. It's hard to explain, but marriage is almost like learning to swim. At first you don't get it, you flounder and kick and swallow water, and then all of a sudden you've figured it out. All of a sudden it's easy. After so much experience and so much thinking about marriage, I knew it would be almost effortless and it was. Believe me, you can't beat finding a woman of intelligence who has a good emotional core and can program a VCR.

It's really wonderful we found each other; we both went through so many years wandering in the desert. My picture of marriage couldn't be the basis of any movie—because all you would see is quiet contentment. Who'd watch a film as unexciting as that? We have our dramatic moments, our romantic interludes, but 95 percent of the time my marriage centers on that warm feeling I get from living with a gentle woman I love and trust. I know that sounds saccharine as hell but what else can I say? That's how I feel.**"**

ALEX SNOW

Forty-eight-year-old Alex is five feet ten inches tall with brownish-gray hair styled in a schoolboy mop. He also wears bow ties, horn-rim glasses, and went to Yale. After graduation he worked for a large New York bank, eventually becoming part of a team responsible for restructuring billions of dollars of Third World debt. He quit four years ago to start a management consulting company.

Alex is enthusiastic but exacting, a quality best illustrated by his sound system: he has speakers the size of a small child and will stop a record or CD in mid-track to point out differences in musical shading and the tonality between different recordings of the same tune. He plays tennis and sails, and recently has taken up walking and bird watching.

His parents are separated; Alex is the youngest of their three children. He is married and has a son and daughter in their 20s from a previous marriage.

Alex's Enchantment...

❝ I married the first time when I was 21; the ink was barely dry on my diploma! I had no sense of who I was and probably wouldn't have done it except she was pregnant. We discussed with doctors whether or not to have the baby and decided, why not? He turned out to be a wonderful son. Getting married was wrong because of my inability to handle it. I was too young; soon I had a family, a job at the bank, and was working on an MBA.

I went from boarding school to college to a fifteen-year marriage, and then was on my own. I enjoyed being a bachelor at 36. I dated all sorts of women—married, single, flight attendants, with all kinds of education, from high school drop outs to Ph.D.'s. Since New York is tremendously cosmopolitan, you can find any kind of woman—Blacks, Latinos, Orientals, Jews, Christians, old, young. However, after my divorce I wasn't all there, so I protected myself by wearing my wedding band. I didn't want to meet a woman who *only* wanted to get married. If I found she was interested *in me,* I told the truth.

I broke hearts on occasion but not intentionally. I never knew I was attractive until after the divorce. I also developed tolerance for the women who adored me and for the ones who didn't, the ones I wished would.

I dated emotionally unstable women: alcoholics, drug users, and self-abusers. An absence of responsibility was what I wanted; I found women who usually had the same goals. Early on, right after my divorce, I had a relationship with a woman who was as crazy as a loon. She's now in A.A. At the time we met, I knew I didn't want to settle down with her; she was helping me lift my feet out of the mud, but in the process, decided she wanted to plant hers. I tried oversexed women but they were really unbalanced and had a pail full of problems. Morning sex is great if you have the time, but it's inconvenient if you rush to a 7 A.M. breakfast meeting. Women like that were enervating.

Relationships can be situational. I was really quite taken by an artist who became quite successful while we were together. I cared about her, but her success—and indeed it had been a long time coming—turned out to be more important than her relationship with me. Fair enough.

It was all a process of discovery. I realized I wanted a woman totally self-sufficient and strongly independent, who had enough control over her emotions that she could look at even the most onerous problem rationally, a woman I could respect. I lost that in my first marriage, maybe everybody does toward the end. Also, I wanted a sense of equity between partners; women I stopped dating lacked this quality. They ended up being limp, never called me; I had to call them and continually make the first move. I eventually started to wind down. I said to myself, 'Is this any way to live?'

I saw Jane at a party. It was the proverbial face across a crowded room scene. I couldn't sleep that night wondering who she was. There was something enchanting about her. Was it was the red hair? I talked a friend into giving me her work number. We started going out. An open and strong relationship developed; I liked her so much I gave up other women, became monogamous. I invited her to move into my loft. I hadn't been there long myself and hadn't had time to finish the items that make a home—baseboards, moldings, a piano. She helped make it ours.

Jane and I lived together for three years and I had the sense that she would have gone on forever in that situation. I continued to be delighted with this woman whose value system matched mine: Protestant, close to her family, motivated to succeed on her own terms. But I had a growing need to demonstrate the depth of my commitment. It was still a big step—although it had been five years since the divorce—especially since there was no pressure to get married. We decided not to have children and there was no financial reason—after all, you pay more taxes when married. I tested her commitment by making sure Jane was around my kids on weekends. She listened to them and took a fearless approach in conveying their views to me, the parent. I liked that.

By the time I proposed I knew about as much as I could about Jane. I also had this strong Protestant sentiment about making her my wife—it's part of my background. So I got down on my knees and said, 'Will you marry me,' presenting Jane with a diamond and sapphire engagement ring. Happily, for me, she said, 'Yes.' **"**

MARTIN RANIERI

Forty-eight-year-old Martin is six feet tall, has salt-and-pepper curly hair, large features, and dark eyes. He grew up on Long Island, got an MBA in marketing at the State University of New York, and moved to Chicago to sell French wines. He now owns a private ambulance company with friends.

Martin hates dressing up: after work, sneakers and well-pressed jeans are *de rigueur,* especially on Saturday nights. He's straightforward and friendly, with a fondness for introducing friends to previously undiscovered ethnic restaurants. He jogs and plays basketball to keep in shape, and is funny and charming in a streetwise, "I've seen it all" sort of way.

Martin's parents have been married fifty years; he's the older of their two sons and is married.

Martin's Analysis...

❝ Nancy was really no different from other women I dated; if I'd met her ten years earlier, we wouldn't have tied the knot. I wasn't ready, but I had an eye out. Would you believe, literally, for *twenty-five* years? Most women I either dismissed as not being 'the one,' or I kept my relationships light. Some went on for six, seven years.

In Chicago it's easier to be single. No one lives in a home; we all live in apartments. There's always good neighborhood stuff going on. I even joined the block association to meet women. Let's face it: I was lazy. If I had to get into my car and drive across town, a woman had to be special. I also kept my emotional distance. Maybe I was afraid. I had my famous line, 'There's no magic.' I know it's a cliché but I used it *all* the time. I was waiting for lightning to strike, and when it did, the woman was usually unavailable—you know, married or seriously involved.

I went out with a woman from Milwaukee for three years, and about the time I was ready to open up, she took off with another man! Can you believe I was blown away? It took me awhile to get to know her; she was gentle but tough, and had some of the same qualities Nancy has.

I found all sorts of excuses for not marrying, but the real truth was my fear of intimacy—plus I didn't want to lose my independence. Undoubtedly, I had a bad parental model: their marriage didn't look like much fun and that had an impact on my attitude. I observed other marriages and never caught a clear, positive message. I come from a large extended family and have lots of cousins, most of whom were married by the time they were 20. They *wanted* to be married. I ran away from that blue-collar way of life almost as soon as I got my driver's license because I just couldn't breathe; I knew I was different from them, and their marriages. I was the first to get a college degree.

Certainly it was a combination of those things and I suffered from low self-image. No one else knew, but I fooled people by being masterful. During my sales career I developed good enough management and selling skills to climb the corporate ladder; however, I wasn't much for taking risks. It took years of analysis to discover the psychological reasons I had for *not* marrying. I'm contradicting myself when I say this, but I don't really think I was avoiding love. I wasn't fighting being married. I just didn't do it. I probably met three women I would have married. Two, of course, were unattainable.

I wasn't interested in traditional 'wifely' qualities. I didn't want any kids. I looked for a companion and a partner. Could I spend time with her? Could she spend time with me? Could she compliment qualities I'm short of? I also wanted intelligence, kindness, and a woman who'd expose me to things I knew nothing about. I've found it much easier to try new things with another person.

There wasn't a list. I looked for women who were interesting, different. Well, maybe I made a list in my head. Women write them down; men have mental lists. Hell, we all have lists, but you compromise. Take two guys discussing last night's date. One says 'Hey, how'd it go?' The other replies 'She has a fat ass.' It's all superficial because if you're comfortable with her, you don't notice her fat ass. Most men don't talk about their *real* list. They'll talk about what she looks like, how she acts; it's not terribly introspective. They go with their feelings first, then sit it out later. Men make a lot of mistakes that way, not thinking the entire relationship through.

It usually took me three dates to decide how much time I'd take with a woman, relative to my other choices, that is. If she were just so-so, I might take her out until someone more intriguing came along. Back to the male conversation. 'How's it going?' 'I don't like her that much, but...' You know, that kind of thing. Men will go out because there's nobody else around.

Women should know this—if a man goes out with you six times, then disappears, more than likely he's found someone else he likes better.

A woman should have her antenna out all the time; she has to pick up signals from the guy. You can tell if a man's interested by the amount of attention he pays to you. Genuine interest. If you go out Saturday night and he calls the next morning, he wants to find out how you feel and let you know he likes you. He wants to keep in contact and he can't wait until Monday. Men who call sooner rather than later are hot, or they're rats, you know, manipulative. If he waits a few days, he's lukewarm. If a pattern develops, say a man sees you six times in twelve weeks, I wouldn't be looking for an engagement ring. Chances are he's seeing someone else as well.

At least that's my experience. Listen, nobody goes out five nights a week, but everybody goes out on the weekend. Saturday nights are still pretty big dating-wise. There are no football games on Saturday night. What else are you going to do? But women don't get it. They wait around for a call or constantly check their answering machines, hoping the guy is going to ring when he's already called someone else. I'm not taking shots at women. They're still not the initiators, they're more the receptors. So half the time they don't know what's going on. So pay attention, and listen—don't read something into what's not there.

In a way, though, nobody wants to stay home on the weekends. Men and women date just to escape their apartments. That's how I met Nancy—at a friend's birthday party *twenty* years ago. She was there with some guy, but we struck up a conversation. Of course, it took us awhile to get together. All our friends thought we were a bad match: too dissimilar. She's nicer, more likable, from the Southwest, and has that certain politeness. I'm gruff and pushy. But in a way, we compliment each other. When I get angry I want to pin the person up against a wall. But she'll diplomatically say, 'Why don't we try it this way?' And you know? It works!

Nancy, like me, never married, so we had kept in touch on a friendly basis all those years. If I'd dated her then it wouldn't have been the same. Nothing is right if you're not ready. Finally, all those psychological stumbling blocks had been removed, and I was ready to take a chance.

But I was still cautious about getting heavily involved. I never lived with anyone before Nancy, except for a few days. We lived together for two years and in that time I found out we were mentally and physically compatible, not that sex is a reason to get married. It's more important when you're dating. When you're together all the time sleeping in the same bed, sex isn't that necessary. If it's good, it doesn't have to be earthshaking. Ah, but when you're dating it's *much* different—after days without physical contact you can't wait to tear your clothes off!

Marriage became a topic of conversation because we were staying in my small apartment. Nancy had already sold hers, so I sold mine and we moved to an apartment with more space. I hate to sound unromantic, but it was also a question of finances. It was easier to get a mortgage. We were two career people working it out.

I never gave a moment's notice to how scary marrying Nancy was. Me of all people. We asked each other if there were any problems. We talked about our careers, how we'd help each other if the other wanted to make a change. That was important, getting our real goals out in the open.

We even thought about leaving Chicago, me especially, because we could do it together. We were two intelligent, mature adults thinking it through. I was 46 and Nancy was 43. You know, I always thought I'd end up married, contrary to the opinion of my friends, and of the women I used to date. It just took me longer to work it out.**"**

JONATHAN POTTER

Twenty-eight-year-old Jonathan is of medium height and of African-American descent. He attended private school and college in Vermont, getting a B.A. in psychology and sociology, before moving to Hollywood. He is a group casting director.

Jonathan has a clean-cut preppie look about him. He wears striped shirts, drives a Jeep, and frequents small movie houses. He's not home much because he spends most of his time going to plays, taking in comedy acts, or networking with other members of Generation X. He's quiet and shy, but has that glimmer of ambition in his brown eyes.

His parents are divorced and he is the youngest of their four children, two daughters and two sons. He is single.

Jonathan's Work...

❝ I have fantasies about marriage after I've been dating someone for a while. You know, things get a little cozy and I think of settling down. I have flashes of living in a house with little kids running around who look like the two of us, taking drives on the weekend...I don't verbalize it though. I haven't reached the point where I am comfortable with myself and who I am. When I do, I'll get married.

I'm really not mature enough yet to juggle someone else's needs and my own. I'm still experimenting in relationships, how I act with women. When I was 18, I'd break up with a girl at the drop of a hat. I couldn't have cared less. I'd tell her 'I don't want you anymore.' I never understood how she was feeling or thinking. A few years ago I reached the stage where I was aware of how much I could hurt another human being. I figured out the dynamic. If things weren't working for me, I probably wasn't treating her well. So I would say 'I don't like what I'm doing to you and you probably don't like what you are doing to yourself.' That's how I tried to end relationships, seeing the other person's side as well as my own.

But don't think it was always *me* doing the breaking up. One woman broke off with me because I wasn't as serious as she was. Another one lived with me for awhile. We had a great apartment and rent was not an issue. Then the agency I was working for lost an account, and twenty people were laid off, including me. Money wasn't coming in and she said, 'Oh my gosh, I need to go home for three months.' She left me.

I have a lot of things to get in touch with, and doing the work is like climbing mountains. After college I was at the bottom, two years later I thought I was close to the top, but the next six years proved me wrong. I'm still selfish with my time because of my job. On a normal day I might be up at 6 A.M. and back after midnight. I used to have the energy to date four people—just a single guy having fun—but now I'm thinking about refocusing and putting that energy into one relationship. Also, my work might slow down next year because I'll be learning the paperwork side of the business, like contract negotiations, that kind of thing.

I have a bicoastal relationship, my girlfriend Elsa goes to art school in Philadelphia. She was out here for the summer with me and I had to slow down a little to pay attention to her. She has the qualities I'm looking for, a mix of independence and nurturing. She's debating moving out here and looking for a job. I don't know if that'll happen but I *don't* want to live together—she can stay with me for a few months. I'd have to give her a deadline: move in September, leave by January. She should know by then what she's doing and be well on her way.

I don't like the idea of living together anymore unless I'm seriously contemplating marriage. My previous experience was intense without any real commitment. My former girlfriend got to me in subtle ways I can't name. After we broke up I felt a bond with her that I didn't know we'd had. I don't want to get that close with anyone unless I'm going to marry her.

I picture relationships like frying two eggs sunny side up. You crack 'em open, drop 'em in the pan, but each stays in their own little grouping. Sometimes they spill into each other. I think people lose sight of themselves and depend too much on others to give them definition. Maybe it's because they don't know themselves. You need to know who you are individually before you can come together with someone else. I'll be at that point when I decide to take a spouse, when I *really* know myself, get further along in my career, make better money. When all those come together, watch out!**"**

Twelve

FINAL WORDS
Male Musings on Women, Sex, Money—and Some Advice

I couldn't finish this book without devoting a chapter to four tantalizing subjects: (1) what men like and dislike about women; (2) the importance of sex; (3) where money—his and hers—ranks; and (4) advice for marriage-minded women.

— WOMEN —

Do men actually like women? Yes. I was unable to dig up any woman haters in this group. I was ready for someone to unearth that *can't live with 'em, can't live with out 'em* adage, but no one did. Men rhapsodized about how good women smell and how good women make them feel. They see women as ethereal and mysterious—so unlike themselves or locker room buddies—and they enjoy the physical differences, the sound of a woman's voice, her whole presentation, her body.

Men admire how much more emotionally open women are, and emphasized women's clearer understanding of relationship issues and problems. They often commented on the lack of competition that exists with a female companion, as compared to a male counterpart. And, they actually preferred talking to women because they're better listeners and more fun! (One upmanship is the game men play when gathered together.)

When I asked what made them reject a woman, their answers were surprisingly specific: Smoking is a *big* negative. One man calls smoking "an outer manifestation of a crippled ego." Another reason for rejection was boredom—either ceasing to enjoy a girlfriend's company, or discovering that an alliance has little to offer, or simply running out of things to say. "Or," as one man put it, "feeling that I was out of sync, like making the wrong choice of a restaurant or activity, not being able to do anything right. She made me feel I wasn't who I thought I was." Women who were jealous or covered up the truth or talked about failed marriages were singled out for negative reactions.

Constant alcohol or drug abuse was highly disapproved of, as is a woman who focuses *the entire* relationship on getting married A divorcé told a story about noticing a pine table at a local fair. When he commented how good it would look in a kitchen he could almost hear the wheels whizzing around in his girlfriend's head: "That means we'll be together—and married—with that table in *our* kitchen." He quickly had to clarify his observation.

— SEX —

Sex proved to be an overhyped topic. I expected to hear: *"Very* important." "Can't get enough!" "I need it night and day!" In truth, men have a more relaxed attitude than I had been led to believe. Ah, another stereotype shattered! As a 27-year-old says, "Sex is important because you think about it about every day.

And it's something people do a lot, so if you're going to tell a woman you're not going to do it with anybody else, you'd better be sure you like having sex with her." That sums up the general feeling in a nutshell. Or as a 28-year-old remarks, "Sex is way up there, but I wouldn't rate it as number one."

Sex is viewed as a poor reason for getting married. Barry Jacobs confirmed that when he mentioned sexually disillusioned couples. And when lovemaking takes on a life of its own, storm warnings prevail. An athlete cautions, "Too much emphasis on sex becomes a psychological burden to the man, who feels he has to perform. When he can't, he worries, and feeling inadequate, he yells, screams, and breaks things."

Surely other factors must be taken into account. A 54-year-old says, "I rank sex in the top five things I look for in a relationship. There are seven days in a week, twenty-four hours in a day. If you have sex maybe once or twice a week, how many minutes is that? You've got to find more common ground than time spent together in bed."

Sexual compatibility was emphasized. So was sex as a form of communication, a connecting factor for intimacy. A 38-year-old observes, "I think you need that initial spark to get started, and it's important throughout a marriage to be physically attracted to each other." Sex becomes a confirmation of the permanence of the relationship—"You don't have to worry that she isn't going to like it and walk away or something."

A 48-old year says, "I think sex is overrated. I used to think sex was the most important thing in the world. A man was together with a woman to have sex: it made him a man. Now that I'm more mature, I don't measure how good the relationship is by how much sex I get. I've discovered other ways of relating—touching, feeling, being intimate in conversation—that have nothing to do with sex. The more I learned about that, the less important sex became."

A guitar player agrees, "Sex played an egotistical role for me. Conquest. I'd sleep with a woman and get very raw and opened up. I'd look at her differently. Wow, we did that? But sex now has to be heartfelt. I need to make a better connection."

It doesn't all have to be "sheet burning stuff." A 43-year-old talks about sex *vis-à-vis* his work, as did many others, who noted that when long hours and late nights are called for, sex is the last thing on his mind. Men talked about sex becoming predictable but no less interesting, like getting up in the morning to fix a cup of coffee. A habit, they agreed, worth continuing.

— MONEY —

The following comments are typical of men's thoughts about finances:

I wouldn't marry a woman who couldn't take care of her own financial needs; she should at least make enough money to support herself.

I want a Republican woman with seven figures in the bank!

I don't want to get into a dependency situation.

It's dangerous for a woman not to work—she'll get bored.

We need two incomes.

I want enough money so that between us we'll be comfortable for the rest of our lives.

I broke up with a woman who spent more than she made.

I see myself marrying someone with a career.

Doesn't everybody have a job?

Less and less do men care to be the only breadwinner; less and less can they be. Men are willing still to take on the larger share of the financial load, but they expect a wife to contribute as much as possible. A man with three children says, "Money is important in its absence; we all have mortgage payment schedules to meet. We both manage to always have almost enough."

In an uncertain business climate when even profitable companies lay off workers, men view women with no money sense or earning power with alarm. As one man says, "How can you love somebody if you can't eat?" That wariness extends to working women who change their minds. A 50-year-old says, "I would be surprised, shocked, and more than a little pissed off, if I married a woman who had led me to believe her career was an essential and important part of her, and suddenly she decided to stay home eating bonbons while I went out to work."

Then there are the extremes—the men who have enough money and "make a great distinction between being generous and being used" and the men who don't, like the artist who confides, "Several women told me they didn't want to get involved with me because if they did and we decided to get married, they'd *have* to work the rest of their lives!"

Although there was much joking and sly commenting about marrying rich, the reality was not as amusing. How about Parker Moses' reaction when his college sweetheart's father hinted at his joining the family business? Not good. But here's an even more telling story:l

A twice-divorced man says, "I had this fantasy about marrying a senile 90-year-old who would leave me millions when she died, six months after the wedding. And I just about found her. I met Rosemary at a party, spent the night with her and thought that was that—until I flew to San Francisco on business and she met me at the airport in a limo. She persuaded me to stay at her house; her children were tucked away with her sister. I said to myself, 'This woman is an easy target.' We went to drinks a few evenings later, where I heard Rosemary had spread word of our impending marriage. There it was: the ultimate fantasy about to come true! This woman was so vulnerable, so open, and was worth millions gained from a divorce settlement. In six months I could have *all* her money. But I couldn't take it. I didn't want *her*. In a fantasy the woman is never there, in reality she always is. She comes *with* the money. The curse of Rosemary, I called it. There's no such thing as a free lunch."

— SOME ADVICE —

Men thought long and hard about offering advice to women who want to marry. Many hesitated, saying they certainly weren't in any position to play guidance counselor. While some jumped right in and couldn't wait to admonish women to "get a life—not somebody else's," others were extremely sympathetic: "I feel sorry for women; there are so many schleppy men out there, I mean real morons." Interestingly, their advice most often echoes that typical of friends, of mothers, of fathers, and ends up sounding like every magazine article and newspaper column written on the topic of love and marriage since *Dear Abby* became nationally syndicated—except that these words to the wise are offered by men experienced with women of different ages, sizes, and temperaments, under countless situations ranging from first dates to last rites. When men freely speak their hearts and minds, common threads and common sense emerge. Here then is their candid advice to women.

Be Yourself

Know who you are and what you want out of life. Respect the person you innately are; don't pretend to be someone you're not or try to fit into a predetermined mold. Men are genuinely interested in who you *really* are, not who you're trying to be. They're attracted to women who care about themselves—we're not talking narcissism here—and who have a "passion," whether it's Doonesbury or rollerblading.

Men can't give your life meaning; they can only enhance it. Let a man stretch to reach you. Men are really turned off by women who fake interest. Don't try to second guess what a man wants. It's dishonest and he'll find out anyway. Besides, bending over backward to please a man is an uncomfortable position.

Learn to be comfortable with yourself. Find out what your values are. Explain who you are and what you expect, because no relationship is going to work if you're not straight.

Be Realistic

Let's face it, we all have limitations. Moi, not perfect, you say? Oui! So, if you're tight-lipped or tend to be reserved around people, loosen up! If you can't resist Dove bars, work out in the gym. There's nothing wrong with consulting a professional: "What should I do about my wardrobe, my hair, my body, et cetera." If you have great hair spend money on it, if you have great legs wear shorter skirts, if you have a great body show it off—subtlety.

Don't price yourself out of the market by being too picky. Thinking you deserve better is great, but who are you turning down? Don't prejudge a man because he's too short or too quiet or doesn't bowl. Give the guy a chance. Even if you have doubts about him, don't be so judgmental. Go out on a couple of dates, then decide.

If things aren't breaking your way, don't *always* blame the man. Could it be you're at fault? Ah, hard to believe! But consider your behavior and how you may be coming across. Do you have a defeatist attitude, talk *ad nauseam* about your ex, or never let your man out of your sight? Are you attracted to the same sorry Casanova time after time?

Don't Compromise

Be a worthy opponent: meet a man as an equal. Discover what's significant to you and make sure it is to him. Be clear about what you want and don't want—and say it out loud. Don't concede on major issues. A woman who wants a man badly might go against her true feelings to jump in the sack with him, but at what emotional cost? Know what your issues are. Divorces happen because couples are unable to get whatever it is they need—so they wreck their marriages in search of it.

Rejection Is Not Always Bad

Get over it. Try not to feel downhearted if a relationship doesn't work out. Sometimes a man knows it isn't going anywhere before you do. Move on. Get used to getting your ego bruised—they have. There will be lonely times and disappointments, but sometimes rejection is temporary—that "wanting my space" thing. Don't take it personally, it's just the age-old conflict between independence versus commitment. Also, don't buy into those male/female ratios or percentage statistics about marriage possibilities; each woman is an individual, not a number.

Don't Say "I Want To Be Married,"
Say "I Want To Be In Love"

Keep marriage off your mind. Don't give men the idea that you have a hidden agenda. Don't enter into every relationship looking for marriage; it should be secondary to understanding, love, and an emotional exchange—not a goal in itself. Would you buy a car if you couldn't drive? If you view marriage as something you don't have and want, whether it's for security or love or direction, disappointment is just around the corner. Men would rather a woman be eager for them, than for marriage. Later it may happen. The trick is to locate a person who matches your relationship needs. For instance, if you aren't strong on commitment, find someone who isn't either. Be open about your vision of marriage, don't get involved in some ideal or fantasy that no man can fulfill. Finally, trust the universe: you can have what you want.

Make Male Friends

Build a close, reliable circle of friends that includes men, especially if you're a woman who grew up without brothers. Men can teach you about male behavior and you'll never want for male companionship!

Meet As Many Men As Possible

Mingle. Try *anything*. Join societies, take workshops and classes with men who share your interests. Sample. You have to extend yourself—men won't come knocking on your door without knowing you're behind it. And realize there's more fantasy in corporate America than women imagine, but both men and women are terrified that getting involved with colleagues will demean and compromise their professional status.

Be Approachable

Men can be intimidated by women, so it's flattering when a woman makes the first move or says something unexpected or outrageous. Be less subtle; a certain level of aggressiveness is necessary and desirable, but the right level varies with every situation. Act naturally. Smile.

Don't Act Needy

Forget about finding the right man—concentrate on being the right woman. Easy to say. Whatever you do, don't be overly attentive, hang on every word, or over-play your hand. It makes men nervous. Turn down the volume on your biological clock and prize your independence more. Don't drop your friends, change plans when he telephones at the last minute, or push him to join family outings. Women with children shouldn't hide them or farm them off to neighbors when that certain man comes to call or drops by for a cup of coffee.

Give Up Beliefs About What Men Should Or Shouldn't Be

Men are easier than you think; don't be so hard on them. Don't enter a relationship with any preconceived ideas about behavior. Contrary to popular opinion men are not aliens or creatures from outer space, any more than we are.

Most Men Are Just Who They Appear To Be

Let a man be who he is, accept him the way he is; you'll have fewer problems. If you want a domineering man, don't push Peewee Herman into being Rambo. You and he will only frustrate each other. Don't ignore what men tell you. If he says he doesn't want to get married, chances are he doesn't. Believe him and go on to the next, no matter how disheartened you may be. There are plenty of men who want to get married.

If You're Not Married, Maybe You Really Don't Want To Be

Think very carefully about whether you really want marriage. Write those reasons—pro and con—on a piece of paper. Have you really thought about what you'll do when a second party is brought into the equation? Can you take away the "I"? Remember, there are no knights in shining armor, although many men try their best to be.

Thirteen

GENERAL PATTERNS

Analyzing all the interviews, I began to see distinct patterns emerge—just as if I had taken a Polaroid and was watching the image take shape with each passing second. For quick reference, I've grouped and listed the patterns discovered:

ON MARRIAGE

- Men want a relationship first; marriage is a natural progression.

- Men hate being viewed only as "marriage objects."

- Men fantasize about marriage.

- Men see nothing innately flawed about the institution of marriage.

- Men admire people who have been married a long time.

- Couples make unmarried men feel left out.

- Men in their late 30s/early 40s feel pressured to marry.

- Men feel they should be financially secure before they marry.

- Men think sex is important, but as part of a constellation of other factors—it is rarely *the* reason for marrying.

- Men joke about wanting to marry a rich woman but when the opportunity presents itself, they rarely take advantage of it.

ON DATING

- Even hardened bachelors hate to date.

- Men most frequently meet women via friends, work, parties, or the personal ads.

- Men don't take women met in bars seriously.

- After three dates, when a man calls you for a fourth, you're in the running.

- Men look for a woman who has their mother's positive attributes, stay away from her negative ones, and mix in other qualities discovered through experience.

- Men are put off by beautiful women.

- Men don't like women to be more than twenty to thirty pounds overweight.

- Women who have been married more than twice are considered questionable.

- Dating women with children (preferably not adolescents) and women older than them is generally not a major problem. Likewise, a different religion or background is fine—but race raises a question mark.

- Men prefer independent women.

- Men don't like women to smoke.

- Men test a woman by introducing her to family and friends, asking lots of questions, creating situations, and then judging her responses.

ON MEN

- Men have a different kind of biological clock.

- Men worry about growing old alone.

- Men define themselves more by work than marital status.

- Men prefer to talk to women because they're more open emotionally and less competitive than men.

THE 27 QUESTIONS

To ensure a measure of consistency in conversations from one man to the next, I developed this list of 27 key questions, which formed the foundation of my interviews:

1. Do you think you feel differently about marriage than the women you know?

2. What fantasies do you have about marriage?

3. What does marriage mean to you? Describe an incident or tell a story about marriage that had an impact on you.

4. How would you change it to suit you?

5. Why did/would you marry? For example, Love…Companionship…Compromise…Sex…Children… Rebound…Emotional Security…Economics…Peer Pressure…Lifestyle…Other

6. What influence do you think your parents' marriage or others had/would have on your decision to marry? How will your marriage be the same/different?

7. Did/would you marry to change your family dynamics or environment (being an only child, redressing a poor/rich background, an uptight one, etc.)?

8. How did/would you determine when you're ready to marry?

9. Would you consider not marrying at all? What would you be giving up, what would you be gaining?

10. What are your thoughts about living together versus marriage?

11. What is your expectation of your role in marriage (i.e., breadwinner, nurturer, care giver, protector)? How does that influence your choice?

12. What "qualities" are important? For example, Physical attraction...Independence...Career success... Self confidence...Trustworthiness...Affluence... Sexuality...Friendship...Kindness...Social status... Chemistry...Flexibility...Lifestyle...Intelligence... Values...Sense of Humor...Other

13. Which of these you've mentioned would you compromise on? Which not? (Would you marry a woman who is overweight, older, with children, much married, different religion, race, background?)

14. What role does sex play? Is there a difference between sex when you're dating and sex when you're married?

15. How about money (hers, yours, both)?

16. How did/would you determine the kind of woman you want to marry? Has this changed as you've gotten older/had more experience?

17. Are you looking for a woman like your mother, someone different, or a combination?

18. Did you/would you consciously seek the kind of woman you mentioned? How?

19. What's the difference between a woman you date and a woman you'd want to marry? Do you separate in your mind "wife" from woman?

20. When you meet a woman who has marriage potential, do you test her (introduce her to friends/parents, take her to sports events)? Whose opinion do you rate most highly?

21. What scares you about women? Does it make you leery of marriage?

22. How did she get you to say "yes"? (Share an anecdote.)

23. How you ever been engaged but one or the other broke it off? Why? What leads you to reject a woman or choose to put emphasis on another relationship?

24. What advice would you give women who want to marry?

25. Would you like to make any additional comments (questions not covered, things not admitted)?

Optional Questions

26. *(For men with children)* What role did your children play?

27. *(For men not married)* Why haven't you married up to this point?

About the Author

A.T. Langford is no stranger to a man's world. As a senior information officer in public affairs for the Port of Authority and New Jersey, she negotiated the typically male domain of tunnels, bridges, and airports.

Her wide-ranging career also includes stints as a workshop leader. "Women in Non-Traditional Jobs," "Dual Career Couples, and "About Rape" are some of the seminars Langford has designed and presented for organizations such as Women in Business and the New York City Police Department.

Langford has a master's degree in personnel psychology from Columbia University. Her undergraduate degree is from Texas A&I University.

A professional writer who's well-versed in relationships—this is her first book, but her third marriage—Langford lives with her English husband in London and New York.